# MARY QUANT

# MARY QUANT

## Autobiography

MARY QUANT

headline

First published in 2012
by HEADLINE PUBLISHING GROUP

1

Cataloguing in Publication Data is available from the British Library

ISBN 978 0 7553 6017 8

Typeset in Bembo by Avon DataSet Ltd,
Bidford-on-Avon, Warwickshire

Printed and bound in Great Britain by
Clays Ltd, St Ives plc

Headline's policy is to use papers that are natural, renewable and
recyclable products and made from wood grown in sustainable forests.
The logging and manufacturing processes are expected to conform
to the environmental regulations of the country of origin.

HEADLINE PUBLISHING GROUP
An Hachette UK Company
338 Euston Road
London NW1 3BH

www.headline.co.uk
www.hachette.co.uk

FOR ORLANDO –

Who taught me to travel

To sleep when bored

To work on planes

To put books and drawings and samples on the floor in airports and get on with what you want and ignore everything else, so I became hugely productive on aeroplanes and preferred it to anywhere else to work because no one interrupted and distracted me, and Orlando did the same.

Orlando taught me to love Japanese food and Japanese style of life.

# Contents

# Alexander Plunket Greene

MY FUTURE HUSBAND, Alexander Plunket Greene, was a 6'2"
prototype for Mick Jagger and Paul McCartney rolled into one. He
wore his mother's gold silk pyjamas and burgundy hipster drainpipe
pants to Goldsmiths Art School, where I was studying illustration at
the time. He had long, silky, jaw-length hair, flopping over one eye,
and frequently clutched a film script under one arm. We met at the
art school's fancy dress ball – I was on a float wearing black mesh
tights and some balloons. APG said it was lust at first sight. I was
simply bowled over.

'Come to Paris,' he said. 'I am busking outside the George V
Hotel.'

It was 1953.

Plunket said he wanted me to call him Alexander because everyone else called him Plunket. So from that day on he was Alexander
to me.

Alexander could draw like Aubrey Beardsley except that his
pictures were more erotic. He carried a jazz trumpet which he
practised on while going back and forth on the train between

Charing Cross and New Cross – often travelling there and back again so he could get enough practice in. He was a total Louis Armstrong fan as well as being a very good player himself. He knew all Louis's riffs and had polished them to perfection. Unbeknownst to him, Louis Armstrong and Bing Crosby were staying at the George V while he was busking outside. Bing sent out the hotel manager to invite Alexander in. They played together, struck up a friendship and Bing invited him to stay. They had two huge suites of rooms and all three became firm friends, arguing and playing jazz the whole weekend.

London was dead. Paris was different. In Paris, the food was better: life was better. In every bar and restaurant the French thumped their elbows, raised their fists and raged, arguing politics long into the night. Politics was fun. French film stars tended to be Communist millionaires and Maquis heroes, making long, angry films. Every Frenchman had a Gitane stuck to his lip, lived on hard-boiled eggs and drank black coffee in dark green cups with gold rims. All French men were intellectuals. They danced differently, spinning you round until you got vertigo. Music was Édith Piaf with Yves Montand in the wings. Even jazz was different in Paris – it was quiet; so quiet at the Blue Note club that sometimes the musicians forgot to blow at all and just kept it all in their heads. Black jazz musicians were the elite of Paris. I found it impossible not to fall in love with the city – succumbing to a besotted state of admiration that I almost resented – because it was so powerful. Paris may be all about the past but then Paris does the past so well. Even its modern architecture was dwarfed by the ancient, venerable buildings of the city, making it seem toy-like and childish by comparison.

Back in Britain, London waited with patient despair. Maybe things would return to the 1930s – as long as no one stirred it. The grown-ups had won a war and lost an empire without realising. They returned to their gardens and allotments and waited while everything calmed down, hoping that life would revert to how it was before the war. For ten years, rationing not only went on but became worse. No butter, no eggs, no meat, no sweets, no transport – yet there was still a prevailing attitude of 'don't rock the boat'. Government control had become a habit. London was a bombsite and the only thing that thrived was the buddleia. Burnt-out basements became jazz clubs or children's secret smoking dens. If you went out to tea you took your own private plate of rancid butter and kept a sharp eye on it. If you had a bath there was a rota and you were allowed five inches of water. There was no heating and no hot water except from old-fashioned geysers that had a fetish for exploding. If you went to an off-licence you were told how many cigarettes or what alcohol you could buy. Young people had nowhere to go to keep warm except the cinema, and nothing to do.

Fog permeated everything. Fog was a smell. Fog was a colour. Fog started in October with children collecting money for Guy Fawkes and did not end till March. It was railway stations and Typhoo tea, Lisle stockings and suspenders. It was going to the Classic Cinema in the King's Road, Chelsea, eating potted shrimps in the front row and not being able to see the screen. It was going to Rules for a big treat and being lost on the way home. It was sinister but also romantic.

We dreamt of America. We knew we had to do things ourselves, or nothing would happen at all.

At that time there were more art schools per head in this country than anywhere else in the world. This ground-level flowering of the arts seemed to have grown out of the Romantic Arts and Crafts movement and was boosted by the ideas of the Bloomsbury intellectuals. Their fear of fascism was proved right by exposure of the concentration camps, which was then rivalled in turn by the horror of the atomic bomb. The government needed scientists but students wanted to go to art schools. Students were not interested in science or politics. They could see where it led: war.

The young were bored and frustrated so finally they started doing things themselves, while the grown-ups groaned and looked the other way. Out of this ten-year gloom burst one great charge of energy, high spirits and originality. Young people started to take control. Art schools and colleges became the hotbed of new ideas in all the directions that make life more pleasing. Meanwhile, the polytechnics produced writers and lawyers who orchestrated the handover of what was left of the Empire. Their elders were too depressed to tell them: 'No, you don't do it like that.' Suddenly, the younger generation seemed connected to an electric current of hope. The new ethos was: if you want it – do it yourself. And what we wanted was art, theatre, film, design, fashion, food, sex and most of all music and dance.

I was obsessed by fashion. I always had been. Fashion anticipates the mood and fashion has shorter lead times than cars or mobiles. As a teenager I spent all winter one year making myself a long fashion chart from Medieval to modern clothes. When asked in a school exam paper which side I would take in the battle between the Roundheads and Cavaliers, I started by comparing the underwear, dress fabrics, colours, accessories, hair styles, hats, make-up, toiletries and demeanour of the two opposing factions, both male and female. I came down strongly on the side of the Cavaliers, as they were more chic. This so stunned the schoolmaster, who was clearly bored stiff with the usual answers, that he gave me the highest marks ever delivered.

I used to inherit my clothes from a cousin who got them first and never spoilt her frocks. I felt they weren't 'me' and I hated this. Little girls used to be sent to dancing classes – ballet classes taught in French, the sort of French that never seemed useful later. But looking through a door at the dance school one day, I saw some tap dancing going on. In the middle of the class was a vision of chic. A girl with bobbed hair, wearing a black skinny-rib sweater, seven inches of black pleated skirt, black tights under white ankle socks, and black patent leather shoes with ankle straps and a button on top – the sort of button you need a button hook to do up.

But it was the white socks that did it for me. Rearrange the focus in fashion and you have something brand new – legs. She was older than me, perhaps eight or nine. The look was everything I loved. I started trying to make my own clothes. That's all I wanted to do. Design clothes and tap dance. And I have never changed my mind.

I wanted to go to fashion school. My parents were dead against it. There is no future in fashion, they said, and from their perspective they were probably right. There was no future in the old ways. Fashion came direct from the top couturiers of Paris, and was produced in cheap copies by mass manufacturers for everyone else. Dior's ultra-luxurious and opulent New Look, for instance, was developed out of a longing for past ideas of female beauty and a desire to sell more fabric – Dior being owned, directed and backed by the millionaire cotton manufacturer Marcel Boussac. The look was so impossibly extravagant and unwieldy for everyday street life that it probably helped hasten the demise of the domination of Paris couture. If I had gone to a fashion school at that time I would have been taken to Paris to see the collections and taught to adapt them for mass production, as that was the way things were done. Luckily I wasn't. But I longed to design clothes. My parents and I settled on a compromise. I enrolled at Goldsmiths.

Goldsmiths Art School was more of an arts club; you collared a table and got on with whatever you wanted to do. The staff were all working on their own projects – painting, sculpting, illustrating or appliqué – and it was up to you to elbow them if you wanted some attention. But the atmosphere was terrific. There were life-drawing and painting classes going on, but what you chose to participate in was up to you. I think there is a lot to be said for this approach. Box ticking would have been laughed out of the place.

Male students in their twenties, returning from war, were older than anyone alive should ever be, through dint of ghastly experience. Meanwhile the teen generation were thoroughly anarchistic. Life drawing exaggerated this distinction: some of the veterans were so war-damaged that they sat on their benches, called 'donkeys', just sharpening their pencils over and over, while other teenage students were producing pornography that they sold in Soho. Quentin Crisp was the most admired model and the most difficult one to draw. He knew it and struck crucified poses for us to interpret.

By going to Goldsmiths Art School I escaped the fashion-school straightjacket. At Goldsmiths, fashion was designed by young people for themselves. It did not occur to me to look to Paris couture. I knew I wanted to design solely for myself and other students: we were our own market. Most art students dressed like Augustus John models, with dowdy skirts and a deliberately ill-kept look, but my four friends dressed like me. Instead of corsets, we wore wide elastic belts at the waist, called 'waspies', with shorts or peg-top skirts like Mods and Rockers, and slick little pintucked tops or tight neat sweaters. Our legs would be covered with knee socks (or bobby sox for the Sinatra fans) or theatrical fishnet tights if you were lucky enough to find a source, and our hair would be tied back in ponytails. Small triangular polka-dot scarves tied sideways, cowboy-style, rounded off the look. We devised our own clothes, making semi-circular gingham skirts you could jive in. Fashion became democratised for the first time.

We were Picasso fans. We loved French films and 'riverboat shuffles', adored cheap French food and Paris, but longed to get to America. We dined on trad jazz and the style of New Orleans, and drank in the new forms of modern jazz and rock.

New ways to dance, new ways to dress, new ways to live.

# Childhood

IN MY FAMILY, everyone's mind worked on very different tracks. My father, a lecturer and historian and schoolteacher, was passionate about music. Every night he practised the piano, Mozart and Schubert mostly, to my enormous pleasure. As a child I was terrified of the dark. I could not sleep because I had to watch the gap of light under my bedroom door, as I knew that pirates would be mounting the stairs, ready to attack. But as long as my father played the piano I was safe. My father's great pleasure was not only his piano but also going to concerts. After a visit to the Albert Hall or wherever, he would sit with the sheet music – not a recording, just the sheet music – hearing the orchestra in his head over and over again.

My mother was a small, chic woman with Mary Jane shoes, Lisle stockings, skirts with low box pleats, and pretty pintucked blouses under neat cardigans. She wore her cloud of dark-red hair loosely pinned up into a soft knot at the top of her head, with tendrils falling down at the sides. She looked way into you, with big china-blue eyes. She was never daunted. Once she confronted two ragingly drunk American soldiers chasing a group of small boys, who they accused of throwing firecrackers at them on Guy Fawkes Night. The local bobby saw the situation, turned tail and ran home. My mother stood between the children and the drunks and told the Yanks they should laugh it off and be on their way.

She had been one of those child maths prodigies. They usually seem to be Chinese or Indian, but no, my normal English mother just arrived at the mathematical answers to any enormous calculation without seeming to work them out. This caused me to abandon maths from the beginning – after all, what was the point? My brother Tony, when he wasn't reading medical books from the age of ten or eleven, would rescue sea birds covered in oil and bring them home in cardboard boxes. Then he would painstakingly clean the oil off and take them back to the beach in Pembrokeshire near where we were living at the time (we spent much of the war moving around the country as evacuees). At a later date he kept part of a human head and jaw to practise his dentistry and medical skills on in the outside loo. Meanwhile, I was busy cutting up bedspreads, trying to make the clothes I wanted. We may have had separate enthusiasms, but we were all mad about tennis and I was lucky enough to have a Surrey coach teaching me. Years later I was called in to play with the male team from Goldsmiths Art School, playing the priests' seminary near Guildford. Nobody told me it was a male affair until I arrived there in the shortest shorts seen by mankind at the time – to rapturous applause from the priests.

Both my parents had Firsts from university and were the prize pupils of their vintage – so there was little hope for us children, as we both saw ourselves as duffers by comparison. But despite this early success my father still felt he had failed. The tragedy of his life, as he saw it, was that he had won a scholarship to Oxford University from Cardiff, something he wanted more than anything else, and then lost it to a rival. My father had been wounded in 1914, which had made it impossible to play rugby, a sport he had previously excelled at. The other young man could. This made my father depressed at times for the rest of his life, although he found solace in music. My mother, understanding this, bought him a Steinway piano with her first earnings. He could not bear to be without that piano or her. My mother had a degree in maths and chemistry and later taught at the London School of Fashion. She could always pick up any sheet of music and sing it straight away. I do think education must have been much broader in their day. They both coached other people's children and older students in the holidays, while we skulked about and played tennis.

My mother's parents were the headmaster and headmistress of a village school, somewhere in South Wales near Kidwelly and Llanelli. They were both dead before I was born. My mother won a local scholarship to grammar school when she was ten years old, and her two brothers backed her going on the long journey and later to university in Cardiff, which was quite unusual for a girl at that time. At university she met my father. Although his family were not Welsh – coming from Somerset originally, I think – they kept a greengrocer's shop in Merthyr Tydfil. Others in the family were coal miners, and played rugby as he did. My father ran away from school aged fifteen or sixteen. He lied about his age to enrol in the army for the First World War, as many boys did, over-enthused by Kitchener's recruiting campaign, which exhorted that 'Your country needs you!'

He was sent to France, flung on a horse and found himself in the battle of Ypres. Wounded in the leg, he managed to crawl back at night through the mud and the trenches. He was told he had gangrene and that his leg would have to come off. But a young army doctor, also a rugby player, had a new idea about dealing with gangrene and managed to save it. Recovering in Nottingham with the army invalids, my father started to study. He made extra pocket money by playing the piano at the local cinema to accompany silent films, adapting the music for the story line. He also played the piano to entertain the other troops, for sing-songs at night. So eighteen months later he managed to go to university in Cardiff, where he was asked to show the Prince of Wales around when he visited South Wales, discussing with him the plight of the miners who were marching on London, and the wave of unemployment that had engulfed the country after the war. My father knew about hardship, too. The family grocer's shop had recently been bankrupted as people had no money to spend.

I am embarrassed to admit that being a child during the war was enormous fun. Grown-ups did the sort of things that children love – making marmalade out of carrots, cakes out of paraffin oil and soup out of nettles. Born in London, my brother and I were sent to various locations around the country to keep us safe. But we seemed to follow the action. West Malling, in Kent, just in time for the Battle of Britain; back to London for the Blitz – don't want to miss anything; on to Swansea for the incendiary bombs; and finally back to London for the doodlebugs. A mad chaotic time, made even more so by the dozen or so schools we ended up attending.

In Kent we were allowed to run wild all over the Downs. There was only one rule: back before dark or they would send the dog out to find us with a message attached to his collar saying 'Come Home'.

Home. Where was it exactly? Even the soldiers of the Kentish Home Guard didn't seem to know. Their field exercises went on all the time. Once, the Goudhurst Home Guard had to take Horsmonden railway station from the Horsmonden Home Guard, who were to protect it from 6 a.m. until 4 p.m. tea time. All of us children were crawling about in the brambles and railway banks so that we could oversee this manoeuvre. Crawling about and getting into things unseen is what small children are best at. So on this hot August day, well supplied with Tizer and scrumping apples, we took a ringside seat to watch the Horsmonden Home Guard sweltering in their thick, felt uniforms, weighed down by their helmets and camouflage and rifles. They'd been creeping in and out the hop fields and oast houses over a five-mile radius since breakfast, quite unable to get to a pub. Back at the railway station, the station master paced anxiously up and down the platform, with one Home Guard in support, and no sign of the enemy.

At four o'clock the London train came in and, armed with rifles and hand grenades, the Goudhurst troops poured off the train, taking Horsmonden station – immediately. With cheers and jeers and whistles, the children tumbled down the embankment, pelting the men with apples and laughing fit to burst.

It was during all this moving about that I developed a horror of milk. The memory of hearing rattling crates of milk bottles being delivered, knowing that later I would have to swallow the sickly white liquid, still lingers. The dreadful smell of milk, the sound of the bottles rattling in the crate, seemed to follow me about. At one school the milk was put to warm on an oil heater, from the beginning of the day until the mid-morning break. I would keep an uneasy eye on it all morning. As it grew hotter, the milk would slowly rise to the boil and then flow over into a large bowl set to catch it, only for the process to start all over again, rising and boiling and overflowing two, three times, the smell growing ever worse. By eleven o'clock, when I would have to drink it, a blanket of thick skin lay on the surface, moving up and down like something on a stagnant pond. I knew it would lodge in my throat, never to go down. Horlicks tablets were offered to help, but this only compounded the misery. I simply couldn't drink it and I would have to sit in a special chair in disgrace.

That whole school was taught by one woman, known simply as 'Governess'. She taught all the children after the infant school, up to the eleven plus. The children would be working at different levels while Governess circulated, whacking their knuckles with a ruler as hard as she could if their work was not up to scratch, sometimes even when it was. When the infant school teacher fell ill, I was asked to teach them myself. I was all of ten years old. I think the idea was that because my parents were teachers, I would somehow know how to do it. And I suppose they were right, because I loved it and got results. The 'mixed infants' were in the old stone school building with a coal fire burning. I would teach the little children to read, all of us blissfully warm, enjoying every minute. It was some time before my parents found out about this, and it was then sadly dropped.

And I was back to the boiled milk.

# Fashion: How It Was

'FASHION' IN THE early half of the twentieth century was the preserve of the grand, not something for ordinary everyday women. It was not seen as a very English thing to do, much the same as going abroad. Before the war it was only the rich and a few academics who left British shores. Upper-class young men were encouraged to travel through Europe, especially Italy, before they thought about marriage. Wild oats were sown and sophistication achieved this way, after a rather wild and indulgent time at university. Girls only went abroad to finishing schools to polish them for a better marriage. In the early fifties you were only allowed to take £25 in foreign currency out of the country each year, and many people did not realise that they could actually go to France with only this amount of money.

As far as fashion was concerned, middle- and upper-class men had tailors, but women's fashion was thought a frivolous extravagance. Quite grand young women had to have their frocks made by aged retainers retired off in the upstairs attics of Victorian-style households. Young women would point out the charms of some delicious dress in French *Vogue* and Mabel the ex-nanny would have a bash at making it, with some heavy fabric bought, reduced, in Jacqmar's sale. The poor girls then had to compete with a chic debutante over from Paris. No wonder our fashion reputation was a joke. In Alexander's mother's family it was thought laughably extravagant that one of the wives went to London once a week to have her hair done. After all, the cook could have done it for nothing – and washed it in Lifebuoy carbolic soap, no doubt.

So Englishwomen always looked best in the country, where masculine tweeds, Hunter boots and fishing hats, or jodhpurs and riding jackets, are so attractive – but they looked a disaster once they dressed up for a special occasion, a ball or a wedding. Englishmen didn't generally mind this as they usually expected to marry a woman and leave her in the country during the week while they visited their London club – and studied the London talent, of course. The wife's hats would come out of the attic and be rehashed for all occasions. Enough clothes for several generations would be found there. Englishmen also often inherited their clothes, but at least they were carefully altered by terrific London tailors. New things were not much admired – it was seen as déclassé, like having to buy your own furniture.

After the war, Nancy Mitford must have been one of the first Englishwomen to have the guts to buy a Paris couture dress – Dior, my God. And buy it herself for good measure. Nancy was an emancipated woman but it shocked her family. So it's not surprising that Englishwomen were generally regarded as being good looking but without style.

No wonder so many British women joined the Wrens, to wear a terrifically chic uniform. We were good at uniforms.

# The South of France

ALEXANDER GAVE ME a beautiful Edwardian umbrella, which became my pride and joy. I took this with me on our first journey to the South of France, while we were still at art school. I wore my black-and-white gingham skirt and black, sleeveless, pintucked poplin top, nipped in by a twenty-three-inch black waspie belt.

Alexander and I had to sleep on the floor of the train corridor, me armed with my umbrella, he with his trumpet. We had only £25 of French currency, which was all we had and all one was allowed to take out of the country at the time. Dawn broke and I stood up and looked out of the window – and there before me lay Provence, just as Cezanne had painted it. I was shocked; I thought he had made it all up, invented it in a purely stylised form, but there it was – dead spit. The train stopped at every little station on the line, all with the most romantic names, hugging the sea as it went. At breakfast time an old man lurched along the corridor with a tray of burnt bread and bowls of ink-black coffee. It was heaven.

We got out at St Raphaël and found a hotel we could not afford. We then headed straight for the sea and lay on a rock all day in that extraordinary sunshine, and swam, snoozed and swam again. We ate cheese and peaches and figs, which we had never tasted before. That night Alexander was burnt to a cinder. He looked torched – he couldn't move. Next day we had to stay in; I smuggled in bread and cheese. The hotel, getting the gist of things, sent up a complimentary basket of fruit with a note from the manager. Two or three days later, when Alexander could be peeled from his blood-soaked pyjamas, we paid the bill and left for Cannes. As the bus started with us on board, a waiter rushed after us waving APG's bloody night clothes.

It was August and Cannes was full – every hotel packed. One kind woman said Alexander could sleep in the airing cupboard and I could sleep on a board on top of the bath. We had arrived in a heatwave. There was a foot-wide square window in the bathroom covered in mesh. I ran the cold tap in the bath under me to keep air moving. Next day we saw from the newspapers that our currency, sterling, had been devalued. We were broke already, with only a ten-pound note left, which nobody wanted. We swam all day and ate bread and moved on to Monte Carlo. I watched a woman fishing. She had a line tied to a pebble with a hook and a piece of bread. She caught a fish and went home.

There was nothing for it. APG went to the casino, bet our last bean and won thousands of francs.

# Mad Hats

ART SCHOOL HAD finished and I needed a job. So did APG. There was a very smart hat shop in Brook Street, right next to Claridge's, called Erik's. A small notice, placed low in the window, well away from the most delicious hat, said: 'Milliners and apprentices wanted.'

I was wearing a three-quarter circle skirt made from Asher's spectacular black-and-white printed fabric, and a tight black pintucked and tab-necked poplin top, which I had made, clinched with a four-inch-wide waspie belt. Accessorised with a swishing ponytail, knee socks and ballet pumps, it was a rig that no one seemed able to classify as day or night. So I pulled up my knee socks and went in.

A small, theatrical man interviewed me, circling round and flicking my high ponytail. 'This will have to come off,' he said. 'You can start work on Monday – three pounds ten shillings a week and you can iron the veils.' All hats had veils then – just short eye veils attached to the front. And very seductive they were. I was to iron the veils into a bevelled shape 'to dramatise the eyes, curve just over the nose and heighten the cheek bone'. The bevelled, curved shape you had to coax out with the iron.

I soon learnt to make flowers as well, using round ball–shaped irons on sticks to shape the petals – a very satisfactory feeling. Then there were the hats themselves, which were wonderful. Each hat took two days or more to make, and would be a copy or variation on a design in the collection. All the hats were heading for Ascot or lunch or cocktails or weddings at Claridge's. Most excitingly of all, I was allowed to design a hat myself, and it sold – twice, three times! It wouldn't stop!

I pricked my finger sewing hats so many times that it occurred to me to use a curved surgical needle, which I borrowed from my brother who was now working at Guy's Hospital. This speeded things up and saved the hats from bloody fingermarks. I loved making those hats – and the hats I designed were terrific. Each to me was a small piece of sculpture that projected a provocative or classy face. The trouble was that if it rained at Ascot, the customers would return them and ask for their money back.

The hours were tough but the smell of cow gum, which we used to stick the fabrics to the mesh base of the hats, kept one faintly high. And on a good day, after a wedding, Claridge's kitchen staff would bring the leftover canapés through the tunnels from their basement to our dungeon. APG was working in Selfridges selling ginghams and strips of elastic for braces by the yard. He had to pull these through a sort of meter, and on a successful day he would reel over with vertigo. He would meet me at Claridge's after work at half past six, bringing a cold leg of chicken from the Selfridges food department because he knew I would be starving and faint on the walk back to Chelsea, if he did not.

So we had jobs, but we had no money. We were staying in Alexander's mother's empty house in Milner Street, Chelsea. One day, in desperation, Alexander pulled out all the wooden drawers in his bedroom and threw everything on the floor – socks, pants, shirts. Some hard square things rattled to the floor. They were huge blue cufflinks with what looked like diamanté studs around the blue stones. There were also smaller blue stud buttons and diamanté to go round the front of an evening dress shirt. Then he found a jewellery box with a Bond Street address on it. APG took the haul to that jeweller and was immediately locked in the shop. The studs were huge square lapis lazuli stones surrounded by real diamonds. They had been left to APG by his uncle, David Plunket Greene. The jeweller thought they must be stolen.

After much persuasion the jeweller threatened to keep them, thinking APG would run away. Eventually Alexander managed to sell these beautiful cufflinks back to the jeweller who had made them in 1930. We were rich. Alexander bought a new trumpet and a wire recording machine – the latest thing. We went out to Quaglino's to celebrate. Alexander was wearing a dinner jacket and a stiff white collar and cuffs but no shirt. He painted the studs down his very white chest and put on a black bow tie. I was wearing my favourite black-and-white gingham check circular skirt, very American in Paris, very fifties. The doorman was stunned but could not fault us, APG being in full DJ.

# Alexander's Family

IT WASN'T JUST Alexander who was different. His whole family was different. Alexander's father, Richard Plunket Greene, became a very close friend of Evelyn Waugh when they were at Oxford together. Evelyn Waugh fell in love with Richard's sister, Olivia. In fact he fell in love with the whole flamboyant Plunket Greene family: Richard the womaniser (APG's father), Olivia the tremendous swinger and dancer, and David the looker, plus their mother, the gothic beauty Gwen, and their father, the trad, pop and classical music singer, Harry Plunket Greene. Not to mention their grandfather, Hubert Parry, who wrote 'Jerusalem'.

Richard and David, along with their sister, visited New York regularly in the late twenties and early thirties not only to have their trousers cut properly (cowboy-style), but also to go to Harlem for the jazz, where Olivia danced her heels off. Richard was a musician and composer himself and also set up a business with sports-car designer Archibald Frazer Nash for a short period. Eventually he married Elizabeth Russell, aunt of the philosopher and mathematician Bertrand Russell. She took up motor racing and won a race in Belgium. This heady brew produced Alexander.

Alexander's father gave him his entire jazz collection, bought in Harlem in the twenties and thirties on many indulgent trips to New York. He also gave us the huge gramophone made for him with a vast horn and heavy arm to play the records. There were needles that had to be sharpened like pencils, and an electric turntable. The sound was much more live than any later developments.

Alexander had a Great Aunt Flora. She was his favourite great aunt, the other being Diana who was a whizz on the stock exchange and spoke Russian, but was rather frightening. Flora, like Alexander's cousin Bertrand Russell, lived to ninety-eight. In fact all the Russells lived to ninety-eight, so you knew where you were with them. Flora Russell travelled the world using the British embassies as hotels since several members of her family were directly and indirectly involved in the diplomatic corps.

APG was regularly summoned by Flora Russell when he was a young man because he was dashing and so amusing, she said, but mostly because of that recording machine. Flora loved making recordings of herself and her relations and friends. Bertrand Russell would rave about the Moscow underground stations, Diana Russell would talk Russian and they all made recordings and ate half squares of black chocolate and Ryvita biscuits.

Flora, having given her London West End house to start the first Women's Club in London, decided to build her 'picnic house' in the country in 1928. Alexander would later buy it. South Down was Flora Russell's dream house that she had imagined as a very small child. Her mother had painted a portrait of Flora, aged six, dreaming of the house. This was re-interpreted as a large portrait painted on the back of the house itself when it was built in the late twenties. The Russells and family friends like the Duff Coopers went there to picnic and enjoy it. They painted, they sculpted, they wrote, made cheeses and kept geese.

Flora used to go to Brighton every August and stayed at the Ship Inn – but slept on the beach on a lilo. By this time – when I first met her – she was already ninety. Her Swiss retainer, Emme, went back and forth to South Down on a motorbike, bringing her little extras she had forgotten. I would go to South Down with Alexander and was much approved of because I didn't wear make-up, according to Flora. Clearly my natural-looking paintbox-and-crayon make-up was working.

When the family first saw me they said, 'Oh my God – Olivia!' because apparently I looked so like APG's jazz-dancing aunt.

# Bazaar

EVERYTHING WAS CHANGING. Chelsea was changing. The young were taking over. London was moving from a place of bowler-hatted politeness – a city of pea soup, fogs, Beefeaters and Marmite – to becoming the swinging London of 'youthquake' legend. Suddenly London was the most provocative and influential city in the world, totally changing popular culture and ideas in the arts, food, fashion, TV, photography, advertising and language, and most of all music and fashion. London became the place to be, the place to work and enjoy life. The voices you heard around you changed from the *Brief Encounter*-style, clipped, polite self-control of the past to the canny wit of the Liverpudlian lager lout. Even the BBC started employing presenters with a regional accent or a lisp. The results were such fun that the rest of the world came to London to join in the longest-running party ever. Everyone came to London and London loved it.

Change, change, change. Fashion and music were the most obviously seductive areas. APG was building his jazz group and took on gigs at other art schools and colleges to make money. He could also cook. I was designing clothes and hats and had been going to pattern-cutting classes in the evenings in New Cross to improve my skills. APG had talked many times about how we could work together. But the threat that loomed over everyone was National Service, which went on as late as 1960. APG only managed to avoid it by deliberately sleeping with the cat, Satchmo (named after Louis Armstrong), the night before his army medical, to bring on his asthma.

When APG was twenty-one he inherited £5,000 and with that he decided we would start a business together with a friend of ours called Archie McNair. Archie had already started the first espresso coffee bar in Chelsea called The Fantasy. He had a studio above it where he employed photographers, including Armstrong-Jones – or Snowdon, as he is more commonly known – to photograph debutantes for their adoring parents. Alexander and I used to stay in the flat at times until we got our own place.

Chelsea and the King's Road was very much a village then, a rather shabby and charming artists' village, more like Paris than most districts of London. Locals went out in their dressing gowns and slippers in the morning to buy their bread from Mrs Beaton the baker's. The sisters working there wore their hair in plaited halos and Chelsea buns around their heads, just like the bread they were selling.

Against this backdrop we started our shop, called Bazaar, and a restaurant, Alexander's, below, on the corner of Markham Square, across the King's Road from the Chelsea Potter pub and next to the Markham Arms. The shop was designed by a student friend and was a very good and simple design – but unfortunately he forgot about town planning and permission. Just as we were about to open, we were told to put it all back as it was, including installing a bay window to match the estate agent's window next door. Chelsea was in a state of uproar about it. To make things worse, Alexander's uncle was a leading figure in the Chelsea Society and lived in Markham Square. There was outrage among the locals, who insisted the original window had been a double bay. We went to the town planning people – we coaxed, we begged, we bribed, I even cried. There was no question about it: if we put it back as they requested we would be bankrupted before we'd even started. We pointed out that there never was a matching bay window but nobody would believe it. At the last stand a newspaper photograph was found showing the Markham Square front immediately before work had started. There was no bay window on the left. The whole thing was quietly dropped and permission given – probably out of embarrassment. Our bacon was saved.

To find a suitable looking-glass mirror for the shop, Alexander and I went to antique shops in the Fulham Road. We found a particularly attractive one with a decorative ornate frame that we painted white. It was a deliciously flattering mirror. However you approached it, it made you look taller and slimmer and more attractive than usual. So we bought it. I have it still to cheer me before I leave for anything important and anxious-making. In the shop it helped sales.

Alexander designed the writing paper and shopping bags for Bazaar. It was the first shop to have the lettering of its name almost the same size as the bag. No one had done this before but of course it meant that all our customers would be walking advertising billboards for the shop.

Bazaar opened in the King's Road in 1955. It went well right from the start, helped enormously by Archie's expertise and Alexander's salesmanship. We gave a party for the opening. We put up a marquee in the forecourt outside Markham House, a bright, gaudy, striped affair with side panels so that passers-by couldn't see in without standing on tiptoes or balancing on the top of upturned shopping baskets. We had a long trestle table loaded with nosh and booze and a burning brazier in one corner to give it a welcoming atmosphere. Some of the waiters from Alexander's restaurant below came up to help.

The party went off with a bang. So did the shop, with customers four deep outside the window. In ten days we had hardly a piece of the original merchandise in the place. The window initially was just backed with hardboard and I pinned the clothes and accessories flat on this, giving a sort of *Esquire*-magazine photographic effect that seemed to surprise people. We then set to work on some white mannequin figures, which were specially made for us by Adel Rootstein and had the right arrogance and pose I liked for the time. We bought hand-made copper jewellery designed by Peter Lyon and fantastic gold jewellery designed by Gerda Flöckinger. The designer Ascher had exactly the brilliant colour – 'Zap' – I loved, so we bought their scarves to sell too. I designed the sort of clothes that my friends in Chelsea and I wanted to wear, such as tunic dresses and knickerbockers and hipster pants, in City-stripe suitings (suit fabrics) and herringbone tweeds. I loved using overtly masculine suiting fabrics and mixing them with fragile feminine textures like chiffon, satin crêpe and georgette. I made hipster pants because Alexander Plunket Greene had his cut this way. I designed skirts cut hipster-style like the pants too, which made them shorter and sharp. In France, Courrèges was also shortening hemlines at the same time. In England they were called mini-skirts.

I needed tights. Stocking manufacturers did not have the right machinery so I persuaded theatrical manufacturers to make us tights to go with the short skirts. (Much later, in 1965, the London-based knitwear manufacturer Swaren Curry offered to do our manufacturing and bought special tights or pantyhose machines to produce them for us.) City gents in bowler hats beat on our shop window with their umbrellas shouting 'Immoral!' and 'Disgusting!' at the sight of our mini-skirts over the tights, but customers poured in to buy.

I cajoled blouse manufacturers into making blouses longer and straighter with ruffle or hunting-stock necks, and we bought these for the shop too, storing them in APG's mother's house in Chelsea. I persuaded men's shirt manufacturers to make old-fashioned tab-collar shirts and we sold them to women, sometimes as dresses or as shirts with pants. I had always been inspired by romantic films in which the heroine falls into the river and the hero (normally Clark Gable) rescues her and then has to lend her his masculine pyjamas or shirt or sports jacket. Harrods had all the fabric resources I wanted and I used these to achieve the look I wanted.

And so it grew.

Some people came every week to see what we had done with the window. Some of them were British couturiers who were very surprised and complimentary and became friends. Alexander usually helped me dress the windows late at night. Once we were arrested when I wheeled props along the King's Road in a pram. I loved doing those windows.

The King's Road became a catwalk for the new mini-skirt, with American press photographers on both sides of the street capturing Swinging London. Life became a running party. The excitement of the Royal Court Theatre in Sloane Square with its new plays, new actors and new ideas spilt out into our shop. As did John Osborne, Claire Bloom, Susannah York, Audrey Hepburn, Brigitte Bardot, Leslie Caron and, later, pop artists and musicians like the Beatles and the Stones, photographers David Bailey and Richard Avedon, film directors Stanley Kubrick and Joe Losey, and models like Jean Shrimpton and Twiggy. Why it caused such heated attention from the start is hard to understand – but the combination of Ascher scarves, modern jewellery, some French jersey wear, my hats, belts and leather pieces, men's elongated cardigans, Irish tweeds by O'Keefe and my own designed pieces caused extraordinary attention. The all-time hot seller that people queued for was a white rounded Peter Pan collar, made in plastic with a press-stud centre. We all know it's the most flattering shape and this detached version was worn on top of plain round-necked jumpers – and did the works. I found the collars in a very old-fashioned haberdasher's shop in Soho and bought the lot. The other wow sellers were my polka-dot chintz knickerbockers and skinny-knit tunics that I followed up in Harris tweed checks, which the American manufacturers went wild for. This outfit was taken by *Vogue* and photographed for its 'Young Ideas' page by the fashion editor Clare Rendlesham.

Some of Alexander's family were horrified by his descent into trade. Not so Great Aunt Flora. Her response was: 'Good, you can sell my hats.' APG had more sense than to say no, so the hat arrived, and he put it in the window along with the mini-skirts, knickerbockers, leotards and copper jewellery. The hat was made of black net and adorned by a stuffed bird sewn on with white stitching – she was rather short sighted. She was delighted with our shop and, hoping to promote us, she bought several M&S dressing gowns, dyed them amazing colours in Dylon, sewed in Mary Quant labels, and left them in various British embassy guest rooms in Paris and Madrid as she went about her travels.

# How I Started

ALEXANDER AND I found a lovely two-room flat to rent down the river end of Oakley Street. Everybody lived in Oakley Street at some time in their lives then and this was perfect. One large room with long windows and a bathroom/kitchen room looking out over the most gorgeous long garden with beehives and gardeners and trees. The bath had a lid so that you sat in the bath with the lid down and had your breakfast, coffee or your work in front of you. The house belonged to a long-time homosexual couple who in order to find us more exciting for them, decided we were brother and sister. They would knock on the door and burst in immediately in the evening hoping to catch us at something sexually interesting. Alexander semi lived there, as was the way.

We bought sewing machines and I started to make the clothes I wanted and did not exist. I went to my favourite store, Harrods, who had the best men's suiting, Prince of Wales check and herringbones and also silk linings and silk satins, ribbons and laces to make the shirts and blouses I wanted to go with them.

I used chopped up Butterwick patterns to achieve roughly the right sizing – I wanted size eight. Everybody was lean then because the wartime rations were almost precisely the perfect slimmer's diet by today's ideas – no butter (2 oz only) and olive oil from the chemist, no sugar, and virtually no meat. I chopped off the pattern pieces I did not want style wise and added where I did. I had been going to pattern-cutting classes. With the extraordinary success of my dresses Butterwick quickly saw the light about my designs and offered me a contract to design for them which I did. These were the dresses that caused such excitement and shock in the window of our shop Bazaar. I went to Adele Rootstein and explained the stance that I wanted the figures, the mannequins, to take. This again was a point that made the city-suited, bowler-hatted city gents so angry that they beat on the shop window with their umbrellas but couldn't put it into words – it was subliminal as I see it now.

Adele Rootstein kept tortoises loose in her studio and they insisted on biting my toenails in my Greek open-toed sandals while work and discussions went on as to the pose. Machinists came every day and collected the dresses I had cut out. This whole production operation moved to Archie's studio where the photographers had worked before, and Alexander and I then moved in to Archie's flat above the Fantasy coffee bar.

The machinists brought back the dresses sewn up next morning and I would walk them along the King's Road to Bazaar, just past the blissful smell of Mrs Beaton's bread shop. Some morning customers were so keen they would grab the dresses from me and demand I keep them for them to try on in Bazaar later. The passion for these dresses was amazing when I think of it now. The dresses I designed were chemise – an easy fit to the top hip bone and then falling in flairs or pleats, often with a loose self belt which sat on the hip top rather than being pulled in clamped round the waist. The sexiness was partly the way people moved and posed in these dresses. The neckline was cowl-like or Peter Pan collared. I suppose women hated the rigid lack of movement in the 'New Look' which was the 'Old Look'. And best of all, these dresses were short, short, short ('Mini'), so legs and an easy look and a mix of male suitings and very feminine blouses under sleeveless dresses provoked male excitement and sometimes hatred – the reaction was all very strange. The hair was Picasso ponytails or Vidal Sassoon bobs and five-point cuts.

Soon we had four or more machinists working for us and I would have to dash back to Harrods to buy more 'stuff' most days, and the machinists moved to the Fulham Road.

Alexander was selling them like mad in Bazaar.

# Alexander's

LIKE OUR SHOP Bazaar above, Alexander's restaurant below was the most staggering success. It became the most fashionable restaurant in Chelsea, if not London, for several years, with an amazingly chic and international clientele. Only a couple of mafia types and some anxious credit seekers spelt trouble, which resulted in Archie and Alexander having to dress up as kitchen staff and pretend to speak Italian like them, so they could lie low and avoid confrontation. These were the years of London's first flowering, so all the actors, film stars, photographers, painters, pop stars and their followers went there. Our policy was not to ring the press after anyone famous had dined with us, unlike many other restaurants, so most of them came back and back.

I remember Grace Kelly and Prince Rainier being there with two friends on table number one. They were flirting monstrously and laying into tagliatelli, which sat in a large basin between them. Their two minders sat at separate tables, their silhouettes swollen with hidden guns, while tackling all the most expensive things on the menu. I was invited to join Brigitte Bardot and her second husband, the French actor Jacques Charrier, and a party of friends, all tucked in at the famous table number one. Bardot was preening herself deliciously as the entire staff – the Italian waiters, chefs and commis – fell into total disarray with excitement. Brigitte Bardot, playing up to this throughout dinner, had no idea it was actually Jacques Charrier they were besotted with.

Such was the flavour of the place that journalists like Anne Scott-James would finish lunch at about 4.30 p.m. Elizabeth David loved the place and never complained about anything. Roland Petit, Zizi Jeanmaire and all their ballet troupe would be there every afternoon during their London performance at the Palladium. Someone from *Vogue* magazine and Audrey Hepburn would be at another table. The new young actors at the Royal Court Theatre would take our debs out to lunch in the restaurant and buy them clothes in Bazaar afterwards – they were salesmen for us, including John Osborne. It was really only Brasserie Lipp in Paris that had a similar atmosphere.

Not everyone realised how fashionable the restaurant was. One of Alexander's aunts came regularly with a niece and shared the 'business lunch' between them – costing £2.60 – leaving no tip. Alexander would rush down from our shop above and square it with the waiters, roaring with laughter.

So, come our first New Year it was with some consternation that we were told that the staff did not want to open on New Year's Eve. With a lot of coaxing and negotiation it was agreed that we would open as long as the staff could wear fancy dress. So with Alexander playing head waiter or host, we sat with friends having dinner, waiting for the expected late rush of customers. The waiters and chefs were indeed in amazing fancy dress but it was only after eleven o'clock that the guests with booked tables started to arrive. Down the stairs to the basement restaurant came an array of the most sensationally grand full evening ball dresses and tiaras, accessorised with towering high heels that seemed to be having some difficulty negotiating the iron steps. Only the unshaved armpits of the ladies gave the game away. The champagne flowed on a scale never seen before. The atmosphere was wild and ecstatic. It was one of the best parties ever given. Only later we learnt that most of the ball dresses and tiaras came from Buckingham Palace and that most of the palace staff and their friends had partied there that night.

# The Wedding Present

ALEXANDER AND I got married in 1957. Our first flat was a duplex, the top two floors, in Eaton Place, financed entirely on our winnings from the card game 'chemy' (Chemin de Fer). Our first bed was a wedding present from Alexander Plunket Greene's mother Elizabeth, who always got straight to the point. It was a big American-size bed from Heal's, bought at a reduced price because it had been the demonstration bed on show and so many people had bounced on it. It was bliss and it has remained with me ever since.

We had no other furniture at all. Financial life was a tightrope. We painted the flat completely white, bought some deck chairs and that was it. No curtains or carpets or frying pans or chairs, just the bed and Alexander's vast wooden gramophone with its huge five-foot-high gramophone horn. Every pound was for the business or a bank or the 'chemy' table that might change everything. The flat was used as a spare studio for *Vogue*'s 'Young Ideas' page because Clare Rendlesham thought it so new to have white paint and no furniture.

*House & Garden* wanted to photograph the flat too and suggested we lay a dinner table. Elizabeth David, the Queen Bee of cooking and writer of the greatest cookbooks, always complained that no one dared invite her to dinner – so we did. She was thrilled. We hired a huge old trestle table and chairs from Liberty's, borrowed knives and forks, plates, glasses and a frying pan from our restaurant Alexander's, and gave her sausage and mash, with the sausages from Jago's of Chelsea sticking up out of the mash like in the comics we all grew up on. We washed it down with lots of Burgundy, and played old original Bessie Smith records on the horned gramophone. The next day *House & Garden* came and photographed the flat. Then Liberty's came and took it all away again. They arrived rather early so the grand journalist writing the story for the pictures said, 'Are you moving in or are you moving out?'

The photographers were wonderful, capturing the table laid for dinner for six with Poisson the Siamese cat – so-called because Alexander won him as a kitten from a man called Fisher over a game of Spoof – ensconced on the end of the table. The vast white bedroom with its white bed and the horned gramophone all featured. When the pictures appeared, old friends were a bit hurt that they had never been invited to dinner.

Wherever we went our bed went with us, first to our second London home on Draycott Avenue and afterwards to Alexander Square, where our son Orlando was born and later moved into the bed with us during teething sessions. It then moved to the country where it became the favoured guestroom bed. Friends pleaded and begged to sleep in it, so successful was it in ensuring total blissful sleep, facilitating reunions and guaranteeing pregnancies.

# Harrods

HARRODS WAS MY favourite store. Harrods, I was told, had the cheapest credit arrangements in London. An account with Harrods meant that nobody got cross about you paying for things for at least a year. Working capital being rather short for our business, Alexander's mother's account, it was pointed out to me, could keep us supplied with the cloth to make my skirts, tops and tunic dresses. I liked to use men's City-stripe suitings laced with very feminine fabrics like satin, georgette, jersey and lace, plus ribbons and beautiful large buttons, all of which were very well stocked at Harrods with its great haberdashery department.

Elizabeth Plunket Greene was perfectly happy with this arrangement to help out and a lot of stock was stored in her Chelsea house in Milner Street. She also gave us dinner most evenings. Antony Rouse, a friend of Alexander's, sometimes came too. I remember a conversation in which Antony politely enquired whether Elizabeth could drive. 'Oh yes,' came the reply, 'I used to drive for Frazer Nash and won a grand prix race in Belgium years ago. I still have the newspaper pictures somewhere . . .'

Come Christmas, Harrods was the natural place to do my shopping and late Christmas Eve the obvious time to do it, as we had been so wildly busy in the run-up to the holiday. I bought all presents in one sweep and found myself downstairs at the main entrance of Harrods with everything brought down for me. After all, I was a very good customer. But there were no taxis – not even Harrods could hail a taxi that late on Christmas Eve. A small boy attached himself to me, offering to carry the bags and boxes for me. It was only a short walk from there to the house in Milner Street, so it seemed no problem. On the way I learnt that he had left home and lived in Harrods; he was a sort of unofficial 'shop walker'. The boy picked up tips helping customers and was known by most of the staff. He had four meals a day from samples and favours in the food hall. He played the musical instruments in the music department, knew all the animals in the zoo by name and had his hair washed in the beauty parlour. He played with toys in the toy department and advised harassed parents and customers on what to buy, outselling all the salesmen and claiming no commission. He was everyone's friend. He was adored by many of the staff in Harrods and slept on the sofas and beds, and generally lived a blissfully happy life there. He took to dropping in at Bazaar when things were flat at Harrods and reported to us about how the business was going.

This friendship went on for a couple of years until his sister found out and decided to join in. She was a sort of streetwise Violet Elizabeth Bott, with purple sweet juice always round her mouth. She had this very small, roaring baby wrapped in nappy bags who appeared to live in a very grand high-wheeled perambulator stuffed with gum drops and fizzy drinks. She would park this with the brake on for indefinite periods outside Bazaar while she begged, which drove our customers away – so our relationship rather fell apart.

The boy was called Jamie.

# The Knightsbridge Shop

TERENCE CONRAN AND Alexander were old school friends from Bryanston School, so Terence designed our second shop in Knightsbridge. There were tremendous style battles going on between architects and city planners at this time and Terence's plans were initially turned down by the borough council because they didn't like anything new. It was not in the style of the shop next door, China Craft, which was a thoroughly mundane design.

The plans were finally coaxed through and it proved to be a wonderful shop. It worked like a theatre for showing my collection because the mezzanine floor above, with its open stairway to the centre of the shop, was ideal for showing clothes on beautiful models with perfect style and legs. With jazz blasting out and all of Knightsbridge agog, crowding around to look in through the very high window, the shop was perfectly positioned on the best pedestrian crossing over the road from Harrods. The opening fashion show there in 1957 was the ultimate humdinger.

We took on a real old rag-trade professional to run the shop, which was probably the best possible idea. Joan could price anybody as soon as they walked into the Knightsbridge shop, just from looking at how old their shoes were and how long it had been since a hairdresser had touched their hair. She taught me all that. She just knew how much they could spend, and she coaxed it out of them. Joan had huge horn-framed glasses, and when she finally left we discovered she was twice as old as anyone had thought. She was a refugee from the horrors of the war. She kept a graph behind her bed with that day's takings and all the details of the days and years she had worked with us.

After she finally retired she took up painting and went to evening classes, had an exhibition and sold her paintings extremely successfully. She was brilliant for us, as all the rest of the staff were very, very young and mostly debutantes. In fact we were overrun with debs: our first sales girl was a deb. Our first models were debs and rich Archie's studio photographed debs. Debs ran Chelsea life in those days and adored our shops and everything in them.

Bazaar also attracted shoplifters; in fact some came back for special sizes and special orders. Saturday was the most vulnerable day, and one weekend Joan pointed out two women to me, working apparently separately, distracting all the sales staff and taking many dresses to try on. One started to pile things into her large bag while the other started a rumpus on the mezzanine floor. Then I saw the first woman leave the shop with her bag bulging, heading up through Knightsbridge. I set chase and followed her into the enormous motor-car sales room behind our shop. Soon the other woman had joined her. I followed and found both looking out from the ladies' loo. They knocked me down and dragged me across the Porsche racing-car showroom floor, pulling me by my hair.

Later we found the clothes and some coat hangers stuffed down the lavatories. They had a shop in East London and apparently took special orders for my dresses. This was not my idea of mass production.

A friend, Percy Savage, came into the car showroom right then and saved me. The showroom, incidentally, was where I had embarrassed myself a few days before in front of the salesmen . . . by trying to order a Porsche two-seater with an automatic gear box, to their horror.

# E-Types

IT'S HARD LEARNING to drive in an E-Type Jaguar, especially when it's the pride and joy of your husband, who is the one teaching you to drive. It was just as bad when I went to professional driving lessons in it. The tutor was so jealous at the thought that I would drive the beauty that our relationship was nearly impossible and he was barely able to teach me.

Shaking with terror when walking to the driving test car with the test examiner, I mumbled, 'I wonder which of us is the most terrified?' The poor man broke down. 'I've been doing these driving tests for forty years,' he sobbed, 'and no one has ever thought about me before.' So he showed me the road sign of a train crossing and a bumpy road and so on, and I was through to my driving licence. It should never have happened.

Alexander had a series of E-Types: white ones, black ones and silver ones. We drove to the South of France in one with me directing when to overtake, as it was a right-hand drive. We drove nonstop with the lid down. As we finally neared St Tropez, we drove through one town with no brakes, as the brake pads had melted in the heat. Despite both of us being covered in flies and dirt because of the open top, we were given the best rooms in the hotel.

The next night at Gassin we went out to dinner and on the way home, turning the wrong way in the road, we had a head-on crash with the editor of the leading Paris newspaper. Both men driving leapt out, shook hands and congratulated each other – largely on having drunk so much wine and survived. I whacked my brow and nose so hard that I had a two-day nosebleed all over the white E–Type. Alexander refused to remove the blood and next day drove into the centre of St Tropez where everyone rushed out and cheered the bloody car, as Jaguar had won Le Mans the day before.

I was taken to a clinic with a vastly swollen face and mega-black eyes. To the clinic's great disappointment, the X-rays proved nothing was broken, but they sold us the X-rays anyway as souvenirs. I lay in bed in the clinic with ice bags on my head while APG read me *Lady Chatterley*.

The French newspaper editor visited and supplied us with champagne and both men congratulated each other again. The editor's wife took off to a clinic in Lausanne and spent six weeks under her analyst recovering from shock, despite having no injuries. The analyst turned out to be her lover. I was photographed by the local press and described as 'over-chic' when I wore huge dark sunglasses while swimming in the sea.

Brighton was a favourite weekend drive for us. In winter we would go on the pier and have a little rifle practice, then head over to English's fish bar and have oysters and Dover sole. In summer we would swim and walk the beach at Climping. Driving back one evening after a two-day heatwave we stopped at a lorry driver's place at the side of the road for coffee, when in rushed a man pouring with blood from a razor slash to his face. I panicked and kept insisting the manager must call the police, which he refused to do, and then hid. Meanwhile Alexander coolly drank a second black coffee at the bar. It became obvious that there were twelve lorries outside with two lorry-driver gangs raring for a fight. The drivers had all switched on their main-beam lights, turning the car park into a bull-fighting arena. Both gangs had razors out, flashing the blades in a lethal silence.

APG, in his palest grey cashmere Dougie Hayward suit, looking chic and toff, watched all this, and slowly took his elbow from the bar. He sauntered into the vast floodlit arena and, pulling a perfect white handkerchief from his breast pocket, walked on to centre stage. Flicking the white handkerchief, he said, 'I say, chaps – what the hell are you doing? Don't you know it's Sunday?'

The entire atmosphere collapsed and there were some slow grumbles and later laughter. Growling, the drivers climbed high into their lorries and, with a swish of tyres, drove off into the night.

We rather limply climbed into the E-Type and drove very, very slowly back to Chelsea in silence.

Alexander was a hell of a womaniser, like his father, and that makes life bumpy. But I was working so hard and obsessed with design, so I knew it was partly my fault. Women would telephone me and say, 'Can Alexander come out to play today?' And I would find little presents for him left in the car. The trouble was he was such fun to be with until he became too ill, and by then one cannot do anything about it.

# Looks I Like Now

I HAVE A taste for moirés and taffetas again. It makes big sleeves and boat necklines and takes clear colour well.

> Silk T-shirts drape the right way and soft silk pants flop beautifully.
>
> Fluorescent pink, red, orange and brown lip colours.
>
> A very purple navy blue looks good, as does a very light navy as favoured by Kate Middleton.
>
> Fingerless driving gloves with fluorescent or neon nail polish.
>
> Aertex and georgette stretches and drapes, and looks sporty and chic.
>
> Leather cricket-pad peep-toe boots do a wonderful job.
>
> A dress over Bermuda-length shorts, both in noisy prints.
>
> Three or four greens put together.
>
> All is colour, colour, colour, although khaki still has its day and always will.

Menswear fabrics are so divine again at the moment; I can't keep my hands off them, design-wise. Manufacturers have at last made fabric just as powerful looking as previously but in a much lighter weight. So we can use men's fabrics mixed with the many delicious floaty, fragile, feminine fabrics, the way I like it.

There is a colour I love which I can only describe as over-washed linen. I like this mixed with very new, sharp, clear fabric. The fashion effect of the TV series *Mad Men* is enormous. I think we saw anew how attractive men wearing hats and smart suits are, and there is a lesson there for women too.

As for make-up, the best development now in modern make-up is the strengthening of the eyebrows. These days they don't turn down at the end any more. This achieves a very flattering curve and gives a slightly more masculine look. Only prune from underneath the eyebrows.

I believe in using a foundation slightly paler than your natural colour and a powder very slightly darker or stronger than your natural colour. This gives a translucent look.

Take the cheek bones slightly higher and further back with any rouge colour: the opposite of the Russian Doll look, which only works if you are aiming to look six years old. Try it – it's as good as a facelift.

Men always know the best luxuries. Buy a very, very good man's shaving mirror that enlarges on the reverse and use it to see properly.

Lipstick has shaken off the excess gloss and the colours are reinforced. In fact colour is what everything is about at the moment.

# The Floating Crap Game

GAMBLING WAS A vital part of life in London. Taxation ran at ninety per cent and you were only allowed to take £25 abroad. For anything more than that, for example if you were renting or buying abroad, after paying your huge income tax you had to buy what was called, for some reason, the dollar premium. I think this cost something like another forty per cent. Gambling, therefore, was the only way left in Britain to have any financial freedom.

Gambling taking place regularly at the same address was illegal without a licence, so we started a floating crap game. This took place in our Mary Quant delivery van so that we could guarantee not to be in the same place twice. This proved to be a very popular and democratic venue, as well as totally legal. Toffs, pop singers, restaurateurs, rag-trade veterans, professional gamblers and rich society beauties all came to our van. Evenings were spent having dinner at Alexander's, then we would move on to Esmeralda's (owned by the Kray brothers), hosted by Esmeralda herself, or four or five of our other most favoured places to dance till midnight, and then on to gamble. Alexander would wear an ankle-length racoon fur coat with a chain loop for hanging it up, which he had bought second-hand from Moss Bros. Afterwards one would go to the Fantasy coffee bar on the King's Road to lick one's wounds.

One night APG won an enormous sum of money – in cash. There was so much that he had to ask Archie McNair to get out of bed and go back to walk him home. Alexander and I had had a major row about the gambling and I had gone home to bed in our attic flat above the Fantasy, which we were living in before we moved to Eaton Place. So APG stopped off at Ward's, the flower shop, and asked to buy the lot – the entire stock. John Gielgud was just arriving for his morning buttonhole so APG insisted on giving him this, then had the rest of the shop exported across the King's Road, up four flights of stairs and into our flat, spreading the buckets and buckets of flowers all through the living room and the bedroom and the stairs. Flowers, flowers, flowers . . . Poisson the cat swung from branch to branch – at last the jungle had arrived.

Gambling took us to Le Touquet most weekends after the shop shut on Saturday evening and we would come back on Monday morning when our first customers arrived. Depending on our state of play, we stayed at the Mercure Grand Hotel or we took a small room above a greengrocer's shop, the only furniture being a bed and a tin bidet. On Sundays we went sand yachting and at about 4 p.m. we dusted off the sandy mud and went straight to the casino when it opened to play for foreign currency. Some weekends we flew from Lydd in Kent. We would travel there in the E-type then carefully drive it through into the tail of the aeroplane. We would then sit up front, having been weighed, so that the fat passengers sat with the thin ones. You arrived in Le Touquet in good time for dinner in the Central restaurant and then went off to work at the casino in your own car.

# The Chelsea Ballroom

APG DISCOVERED THE most perfect flat in Chelsea, five minutes from Bazaar and all the fun of the King's Road, and five minutes from the office studio in the garage in Ives Street. The Draycott Avenue flat was on the first floor and had once been an enormous ballroom with fabulous parquet flooring. This became my studio by day and party venue by night.

Alexander had a raised platform made at one end where we put a handsome Swedish porcelain stove, with long bookcases on either side and two large, scarlet leather sofas facing each other, north and south. This place is now used as a very exciting art gallery. There was a bedroom with huge, handsome, built-in cupboards and a brass library rail and ladder. A chef's kitchen was built, in which you could reach everything while standing centrally. APG had rush matting, very new, installed everywhere except the ballroom and the kitchen. The bath was very handsome with a huge mahogany rim and brass feet, found for £5 by the men working on our flat. They painted the inside of the bath, left it full of cold water for four days as directed, and then, with great ceremony, we all collected to pull the plug. Unfortunately they had forgotten to connect the drainpipe and the whole bathful of water fell through the floor, on to a rather valuable grand piano and Aubusson carpet in the ground-floor flat below.

Terry Donovan found us the most enormous, handsome refectory table from a nunnery in Wales and this became my workplace, littered with drawings, Copic pens and samples. The only other furniture was a huge Spanish cupboard kept full of wine, a target for pistol practice and a bicycle I had won for some reason, which was useful for racing around the ballroom. At night the ballroom held dinner parties and pop and jazz groups performed on the dais. Our vast horned gramophone sat in one corner while Poisson the cat skated about, chasing Brussels sprouts.

Unfortunately, what with Simone Signoret, Violette Leduc, American *Vogue*, George Melly, Lulu, Dudley Moore, Michael Caine and other unmentionables dropping in, our Draycott Avenue flat turned into one of the most popular apartments in Chelsea and thus it became more and more difficult for me to use it as a workspace and to concentrate.

The place was a dream for parties and a dream for television crews, who would not leave us alone. American and British TV had found the perfect plot and with it the perfect base to showcase the London scene. One night Jonathan Miller and the *Beyond the Fringe* people, American *Vogue*, Jackie Kennedy's sister and French *Elle* were gathered at ours for a party to celebrate and transmit the first cable TV recording. Unfortunately it took so long to set up, that by the time they were ready to shoot – after we had been forced to be there on hold for ten hours – everyone was drunk. The full-length windows were covered in yellow paper for some reason and four months later a six-inch nail was found lodged in the main fusebox to the building to avoid breakdown. Despite all that, the recording of the party managed to be transmitted, bouncing directly across the Atlantic for the first time.

Our amazingly speedy success in the King's Road left us as stunned as everyone else. We couldn't quite believe it, or cope. Our banking, for instance, was done when the till drawer would not shut any more. Bazaar became a friendly meeting place for actors, musicians, photographers, models and film directors – an outrageous day-and-night party that we gaily attended while privately we worried to death as to how we could support it financially. The press naturally could not stay away from such a place.

It was not surprising therefore that there was some sour grapes from some quarters – especially France. I think the press were so amused by Chelsea having so much attention that they kept asking French couturiers: 'What do you think of the Mary Quant success?' which did not help matters. At the same time, many young French people were discovering what life was like in London with French reviews of its theatre, clubs and even restaurants. I see now that I should have been flattered by so much French and American press attention. The Americans loved it – it was something young and new – but the Paris couture world did not like all this attention going to London and a British designer. So when the press told Coco Chanel that I admired her beyond all others, she said, 'From her, it is a very small compliment.' I don't blame her. Other French couturiers said my designs were vulgar or gimmicky and some said I was 'a flash in the pan'. I began to call myself a flash in the pan, but I was in fact pretty upset.

Over the years I have come to see that 'new' is often described as 'vulgar' by people who are frightened of change. I had demonstrated that from now on fashion was going to be mass-produced, that the future did not lie in the laboriously hand-sewn designs that were the hallmark of couture. Even then I was designing for mass production, for a young mass audience, leaving behind that aura of sadness that clung to the world of haute couture, where seamstresses would work in a dungeon for two or three days to make *one* hat or *one* dress for *one* woman, who may or may not wear it, a melancholy that somehow shows in the final couture dress. My designs had an ease and a lightness and a different sort of polish. They spoke to a different audience. The best mobiles and iPods have it today too.

Meanwhile, the pressure of celebrity was very puzzling to handle. Sometimes I felt it was a tease and I wanted to hide or run away from it. But at the same time I enjoyed it and wanted to use it to help me in my battles with the manufacturers that I needed to make the clothes and products that I wanted.

The attitude of manufacturers in the fifties and sixties towards designers was resentful. They didn't want to employ designers or have them point out what to make. Manufacturers liked others to test design ideas and then if they sold well the manufacturers would copy them. So they looked through magazines and pointed out the good sellers and made those cheaper. 'Who needs designers?' was the view. They were simply upstart art students to be avoided at all cost. There were even rumours of designers being paid not to design because they were good and that was worrying. It meant power lay in the wrong place in business.

# Andrew Loog Oldham

ONE DAY THIS sixteen-/seventeen-year-old boy came into my office demanding to be taken on. He was followed smartly by his mother, who begged me to take him on as an assistant – anything – as she could not deal with him and he would not go to school.

The boy was dressed in an Edwardian suit and carried a walking stick with a silver top. He was there, outside, every morning in the King's Road, until I took him on, to help carry things about for window displays, deliver things and so on. As he would say: 'And anything else?'

At night he worked at Ronnie Scott's, so he would telephone Alexander and me late at night if any really exciting American jazz player came in, as they often did. We would get out of bed and go.

Nine months later he resigned. Writing from Dover on the boat to France, he thanked us politely, explaining that now he could do any one of our jobs standing on his head so he thought he had better resign. Six months later the boy, Andrew Loog Oldham, was managing the Rolling Stones, which seemed a pretty good recommendation for our training.

# Chat

I WAS QUITE shy, except for moments when my diffidence had been mistaken for nothing to say, and a verbose arrogance took over. To defend my designs or products I would suddenly become terrifically fluent. This amazed me, as I did not know when one character would overtake the other. The cure for my shyness was found in a press conference in America when a journalist asked me: 'Tell me, Miss Quant, what is this shy thing? Is it the new fashionable style in England?'

With a flash of insight like a slap across the face, I realised he was right: shyness was an act. I have never been shy since, and it seems nobody else is either. It was a pre-sixties affectation, since blown out of existence, probably by John Osborne. The *Look Back in Anger* actress Mary Ure had it – she was shy and demurely charming, but refuse her a table in Choys, the King's Road Chinese joint, and she could throw a switch and become the actress, the star. Naturally a table would have to be found.

I found my first television interviews a terrifying ordeal. I would arrive early and be put into a clinic called 'Make-Up' for about an hour, where they would cover me in orange panstick, red lipstick and very white powder, making me quite unrecognisable. If I tried to demure I would be told: 'Television is different; you have to wear make-up.'

Next, I would be positioned for rehearsal, and elaborate chalk marks would be drawn round my feet, from which, I was told, on no account must I move. Rehearsals would start, and I would be interviewed over and over again and told to remember to say this or that, again and again. Gross anxiety would crackle like electricity in the air around the professionals, adding to my own, while huge cameras on trolleys and tracks would loom up at me.

Recording would start with a clapperboard threatening my nose. Three or four sessions would be rehearsed again, before the word 'Live' would freeze me. Several of these 'Lives' would be repeated because something showed – a chair, a shadow, the microphone, a streak on my nose. More powder would be administered and then it would be 'Live' again. By this time my quotes had become rhetorical questions for the interviewer and my voice would have taken on the clipped tones of Celia Johnson in *Brief Encounter*. I was reduced to a pancake.

Very stiff drinks would be produced in the hospitality room – or recovery room as it should have been called – and I would leave, knowing I had embarrassed and appalled everybody, especially myself.

British television suffered from having a literary background, whereas Americans ploughed straight in. Americans were talkers. Americans were salesmen. The British made speeches from paper – even politicians did until quite recently, when they watched Clinton.

Now all Britons can speak and make presentations and can't be stopped. But it was *That Was the Week That Was* that cracked the mould on TV.

The Japanese have a completely different view about chat. They don't go in for it at all. A picture of complete contentment is a group of Japanese people sitting and eating together and not saying a word. Whereas the fastest way of achieving information from a Westerner is to force a long silence. They simply can't take it.

I did eventually improve at speaking in public. One time I was asked to talk at an event with various other luminaries, hosted by Cherie Blair. The speeches were so long-winded that when it came to mine I made it very short and precise. Bono said to me, 'My God! You talk in sound bites!'

I was rather pleased with that.

# Heart-Shape

THERE IS A vulnerable moment towards the end of a long interview when you really are exhausted and just longing to get out. Journalists must know this because that's when the killer question usually comes. One day in the early sixties I was asked, 'Why are women so preoccupied with fashion and make-up?'

I replied, 'Well, yes we are, it's part of being female and even if we did not wear clothes, we would decorate ourselves, as you can see historically. For instance I encourage Alexander to trim my pubic hair into a heart-shape.'

Well, the sirens went off and when the interview appeared the whole piece was devoted to this quote. It ricocheted everywhere. Strangers in pubs and restaurants bought me a drink on the strength of it. John Lennon adored it and started sending me various ideas of other shapes I could try. I had known him since he bought his black leather cap and other items from our shop. We met in clubs and were affectionate friends until foreign press gossiped of an affair, which sad to say, as in the case of the dashing French actor Jean-Paul Belmondo, was unfortunately not true. But he did send me messages of huge encouragement when I was in danger of miscarriage at the same time as Yoko Ono. He was a very sweet and often depressed man. I once sat next to him at a literary lunch at Foyle's to launch his book of rhymes and doodles, *In His Own Write*. He was paralysed with fright at having to speak at this literary haven. A horrid bully of a man stood up and said how disgracefully rude and insulting it was of Lennon not to speak. I was furious and clutched John's shaking hand. He was near tears with frustration and embarrassment.

My heart-shaped pubic hair seemed to rivet both the people and the press. Some years later, APG and I spent a weekend in Brighton, a favourite escape haunt, and with several friends we went to a new Italian restaurant. It was a blissful heatwave of a summer and we all decided steak tartare would be just the thing. The food arrived beautifully presented – but mine failed to show. Ten minutes later my steak tartare finally arrived, carefully crafted into a heart-shape. It takes an Italian waiter to have such romantic finesse.

# What I Learnt in the Sixties

MY BEST MEMORIES of the 1960s are ones of optimism, high spirits and confidence. You are more likely to get a design right if you are typical of the market you are designing for, plus I had the great advantage of being female. I could try things out myself, I knew how things felt and I road-tested my own designs and make-up.

I realised you have to feel design and colour passionately and trust your instinct, often in the face of powerful men who have different ideas but who you need to manufacture and market for you. Fashion only becomes commercial when it's right for the time, which means it should be a little ahead of the time, but not too much.

The more ideas you design, the more you can produce, as long as you remember that fashion has to please both sexes. You have to persuade, seduce and convince both the people selling fashion and the people wearing it. Men selling and marketing cosmetic ideas for you need to know and experience for themselves the difficulties of applying make-up as well as merely admiring the effect. This leads to great fun but is seriously valuable when you think of the importance of mascara brushes and applicators in achieving a finished look. This made me persuade our people to train young men as well as women to be demonstrators.

Any salesmen baulking at this idea should be reminded of a story that the former MD of Mary Quant Cosmetics, Brian Baldock, used to tell of his days as a young salesman. One time, when faced with a stubborn supermarket manager who refused to buy his products, he actually opened a can of dog food and ate it with relish to prove the quality!

While I was growing up one of the favourite phrases said to children was, 'You wait until you're grown up, when you have to face real life.' This made me want to avoid 'real life' and live a sort of fantasy life. In many ways this is what has happened to me.

# Inspiration

I AM OFTEN asked where inspiration comes from for a designer.

For me ideas come from everything. Everything I see, read and think about. The way a scarf is tied might become a skirt. A skirt might become some pants, a top might become a coat. A boot becomes a dress, a bandage a hat. I seem to have the mind of a vacuum cleaner – but the pieces all turn into something else and one design turns into another. Tying and bandaging is very relevant. But zip fasteners and even rubber doorstops can also be inspiring.

There was a shop in London that sold nothing but chefs' and waiters' outfits. Most of it was white or black plus there were several long, striped butchers' aprons. When walking past I thought, 'How smart – I must have some of that.' I knew the fabric would make great mini-skirts and tunics and Capri pants for us. I designed a whole collection with it.

Another great source of inspiration to me was Edwardian underwear, both children's and adults'. I used to go to the V&A to find a peaceful place to work and found lots of ideas there as well. I loved children's Liberty bodices, bloomers and buster suits (shorts buttoned on to a top for boys), camisoles and combinations. I was also fascinated by men's shirts with tab necks and detachable collars, double-backed men's shirt cuffs, channel seams, and arrowhead or sprat's head tailoring stitches, which can be used to reinforce and decorate the end of a seam or pleat. My favourite technique was to run a channel seam down to just above crotch level, finished with a sprat's head and bursting out below into centred fan pleats.

It is fun to me that this sort of sexiness is not usually analysed.

# JC Penney and 1,765 Stores

THE JC PENNEY proposition was the most extraordinary project put to us, and certainly the most influential one for me. It is difficult in retrospect to see how unlikely it was at that time for the largest retailer in the USA to approach me to design a collection for them in 1960. So when Paul Young, a buyer for JC Penney, stepped through the Alice door in our garage in Chelsea, which we used as an office and studio, it is not surprising that we thought he was joking and told him to buzz off. When it became clear the project was serious we decided we must go to America to find out more about JC Penney.

Old man Penney rightly had a great reputation in America. He had started with one store out west with his wife and their baby, who was kept in a drawer under the counter. The first employee he trained, he put in charge of his second store and so on until he had developed this enormous group of 1,765 stores. He was said then to have hit the bottle, but later recovered. As a result, no employee of his was allowed to drink or be divorced. By 1960 this had become rather difficult to police, but despite no employee ever leaving their hotel room sober during a business trip, they were never seen to drink.

By the time Paul Young came to see us, Penney's stores were trustworthy and reliable, but also a little dull, a little old-fashioned. Customers were turning to other brands. Paul Young, a particularly bright young man in quite a junior position in the buying office, had been chosen to tour Europe for six months, get ideas for young people and come back with something unusual enough to cause comment and arouse new interest. He'd already visited France, Italy and the Scandinavian countries before he'd hit London. He'd seen some of our publicity after our first trip to the States, and wanted to come over and take a look at what we were doing. When he saw the clothes I was working on he got frightfully excited. He asked if he could put a call through to New York. We heard him say, 'I have seen this person in Paris, this one in Italy, this one in Spain, but there is nothing to touch Mary Quant. I absolutely believe that our whole project should be launched on this girl. Forget about the European promotion. This is it.'

Our next step was to ask the advice of the two 'Queen Bees' of America, fashion journalists Eugenia Sheppard and Sally Kirkland of *Life* magazine – two telephone numbers given to us by our friend, the fashion PR Percy Savage. They were said to have taken to their beds with hot towels round their heads for a weekend to deliberate such an extraordinary and dangerous proposition. Apparently it could be death of a designer, or was it the future? They decided, yes, it was the new way to go. For me, America was where I learnt, more than anywhere else. With JC Penney's buying power and scheduling I was able to spread my designing into dresses, sportswear, bedwear, hosiery and underwear. It was like designing for Marks and Spencer – which I did do later – but with my name on it, which Marks and Spencer would never do.

Working for JC Penney was my most successful and gratifying design experience as the top American fashion manufacturers were in such awe of their buying power – so for me it was like being President or Margaret Thatcher. American manufacturers were prepared to make anything for me, find anything, dye any colour, match any ribbon and dash all over New York to develop the samples for JC Penney just the way I wanted. This was heaven after Britain, where some manufacturers would not take my demands seriously as they thought I was too young – as a result of the mini-skirts and over-the-knee socks I wore, no doubt. In New York we could produce sixty or seventy new samples, costed and duplicated, in one week – beautifully sized, finished and shown for JC Penney from my designs.

The launch of the collection in 1962 was to be in the British Embassy in Washington, attended by the British ambassador David Ormsby-Gore and his wife. Old man Penney himself was hosting the event and arrived in his personal aeroplane wearing a Stetson hat with a plastic wrapper press-studded to it. The hat was never removed from his head inside or out of the British Embassy. He was a marvellous presence at the high table with all his top executives ranged on either side of him, and he spoke for three-quarters of an hour to all the fashion press of America about living a pure life and abiding by the golden rule, 'Do unto others as you would be done by' (his first shops were called the Golden Rule Stores). The entire lunch and fashion show was teetotal, although the Ormsby–Gores had thoughtfully brought us some neat vodka in water bottles.

The launch may have been dry but the Mary Quant collection was a hit.

After that came the promotion: the TV, the tour, the song and dance. First the TV. I arrived and was waved into a studio, then signalled to go straight into a session where the interview ahead of me was going on, *live*, and without stopping I was encouraged to join in. Lighting up a Gauloise to control the nerves, I was told on camera it would be better not to smoke and to stop fiddling with the microphone. I said, 'But I must have something to do with my hands – I must have a fag.' The whole studio and all the cameramen erupted into riotous laughter. 'Oh my God – fag!' said Barbara Walters. I didn't know what 'fag' meant in America.

We recruited some of our favourite models for the trip across America, including Amanda Lear who was the muse and friend of Salvador Dali. Double rooms had been booked so that the models shared with each other. (Sounds like footballers nowadays.) But a great whispering campaign started up amongst the girls: 'I am not sharing with her [Amanda Lear] – she is a man.' APG, who was organising the trip from the London end, went into panic about this conundrum and decided to delegate the delicate problem to my PA. There had always been rumours about this. I always suspected they were put out by Amanda herself, as she had a taste for fun. She also said she took the vet's prescription for calcium tablets as dogs know a thing or two about bones. Amanda was certainly tall and had the right bone structure. She was a terrific model and cabaret star in Paris. Of course, as the trip progressed there were outraged squabbles amongst the other girls, who were saying, 'It's my turn with Amanda!' 'No, it's mine!' She was certainly very female and witty and once told me she'd slept with Sammy Davis Jr, who we met on the trip. He certainly gave us the best table and seats for the performance we saw while we were in the USA.

Amanda later said she slept with Sammy in order to find out whether he took his glass eye out in bed. This reminded me of the aftermath of a party we gave in our Chelsea ballroom flat. When clearing up in the morning we came across a glass eye. I've always wondered whether it was his.

Another wonderful model on this trip was underage and her mother rightfully came and vetted Alexander before we set off. I don't know how she arrived at her conclusion to OK the tour, but this girl was allowed alcohol on the aeroplanes and bars across America whereas I was always judged to be underage and therefore not allowed to drink. I was so flattered by this verdict that I went without alcohol for some time until it became unbearable. Alexander had to bring a travelling bar everywhere with us so I could get a drink.

The shows were a terrifying success. There was something about the way our girls, debs, danced – in leggy mini-skirts with their Vidal Sassoon-bobbed hair flying – that really got America excited. At the time, young American women still dressed to look like Barbara Stanwyck or to look as frightening as possible, whereas we all looked about sixteen and never stopped dancing, with a mix of jive, twist and rock and roll. The models who worked with me were also very grand and classy, which confused American thinking. There was this appetite for life that simply poured out of us, an extraordinary zest for independence, travel, music, food and sexiness that we all seemed to bring with us from London. 'Say "super",' Americans would say to us and so we did.

At the end of the shows, fifty or sixty girls would besiege our hotel, blocking the entrances to our rooms, demanding Vidal Sassoon-style haircuts from us before they'd let us pass. So I am sorry, Vidal, but the models and I did as best we could, there and then in the corridor.

Putting on dress shows at the rate of a city a day and dancing across America with twenty-eight suitcases, a pop group (The Skunks), seven models, Alexander, my PA and me, was all enormous fun but enormously exhausting too. We never ate and arrived so late in hotels and left so early there was only the bedroom's Nescafé and biscuits for sustenance. Arriving in Las Vegas to check into an unbelievably large hotel, we found we had a vast suite of gigantic rooms with fruit machines next to our bed and in the bathrooms. I walked around pulling the cords of the heavy floor-length curtains and had a claustrophobic breakdown. There were no windows, only concrete walls. Between the hotels and casinos was only desert. One model and I went for a walk into the desert and a helicopter arrived to winch us up. No one ever went for a 'walk' in America.

Our shows changed the whole way fashion was presented. Before we came, fashion shows were still modelled by paralysed-looking middle-aged women in corsets and frozen 'beehive' hairstyles, with male presenters who would say, 'Here comes Melissa in a pale blue dress with un-pressed pleats in Missy size eleven,' as though you were blind. Now three thousand people turned up for our wild fashion shows, with models dancing, a pop group playing and the police and fire brigade arriving in a blind panic.

While these fashion shows progressed I was still sending back drawings and messages to the studio in the Fulham Road for the next collection. It was unstoppable.

That first foray was just the start. Thanks to JC Penney I began commuting to New York once a month. The Algonquin became our home in New York, as it was to many London theatre people such as Peter Cook and Kenneth Tynan. The valet there became a great friend and would do alterations to fit different models for me and report back what journalists and buyers said in the lift if they came to see the collection there. On one visit with a very tight schedule I had appalling flu, which developed into bronchitis. I had to make the appointment with a raging fever. The Algonquin called in two doctors day and night and ice-cream was sent up to my room every hour. I realised then that a good hotel is the only friendly place in which to die – room service and champagne will be sent up and they will deal with the corpse if they need to, but they will aim to keep you alive as long as possible because they don't like the publicity.

Some of the collections I designed for JC Penney were surprisingly dressy and were some of my best. One collection used black moiré for mini-dresses with white pintucked cotton bibbed fronts, and featured mini-skirts with braces and contrast-coloured skinny rib sweaters. The JC Penney team were marvellous to work with. I suppose, like many men at the time, they were so surprised and shocked by the mini-skirt fashion revolution that they rather stood back and let me get on with it.

I was persuaded to help advise the chain on underwear, as the entire JC Penney buying force for women's undies was male. I persuaded them that providing a full range of tights/pantyhose, which they previously barely stocked, was vital for the company if they wanted mini-skirts to sell in a big way. This strategy was so successful that they turned all their hosiery buying power towards pantyhose, and were so well positioned to persuade American hosiery manufacturers that tights were the future that they reaped the rewards of this decision alone for years. They made millions, and true to old man Penney's word, they abided by their golden rule, insisting on paying us a huge fee as well as the royalty for what we had done for them.

I later persuaded them to make more naturally shaped bras. Somewhere there exists a photograph of me, very small and mini-skirted, lecturing these very charming large American men about the shape of breasts. I remember, with some embarrassment, quoting Colette to them: 'Breasts are shaped like half a lemon – the interesting half. They are not tennis balls.' And so we arrived at very soft preformed fabrics with underwired structure and other natural-shaped bras to achieve what was called the 'No–Bra' bra effect. This was the era of bra burning and student riots in California.

Travelling across the Atlantic so much, I became very aware of the 'house-wear' market in the USA. This encouraged me to design a collection of jersey tops and hotpants in striped jersey-knit fabrics with matching bras, pants, socks, leg warmers and minis – all using knitted fabrics of various thicknesses and weights. I loved them and so did the market. But stores in Europe were bemused as to which department to sell these in. Was it hosiery or knitwear or what? We also manufactured these garments very successfully in Germany. As I love breaking down barriers all this was great fun. Quite soon this collection was promoted as 'underwear as outerwear' and vice versa. It all worked wonderfully with tights and different patterns and textures.

One of my favourite memories is of showing these incredibly lightweight undies in Frankfurt at the deadly serious underwear trade fair. We had the top, most exquisite photographic models dancing to the Supremes' 'Baby Love' recording, disrupting the entire trade fair. Everyone came to see. The rest of the fair consisted of stout middle-aged models showing stays and corsets – so you can imagine the chaos that ensued.

Later trips to America took place in the wake of the Beatles, with two of the Beatles' girlfriends (Patti Boyd and her sister) modelling for us. Alexander was hounded down by a mob in the street who insisted he was Paul McCartney. APG and I managed to go out to dinner alone one Sunday night and after dining they refused to give us a bill, but instead insisted he sing. For once Alexander refused but if he had brought his trumpet then I'm sure he would have done. Alexander became a disc jockey on local radio stations across America, advertising the fashion shows, and had his own fan club known as the Junket Creams. He was often asked to read the news – English accents were in. He had to read the news the day that my aeroplane had been struck by lightening and had turned us upside down.

The Mary Quant collections for JC Penney were so successful, I went on designing for many years for them until I became pregnant again after a heartbreaking miscarriage. In retrospect I am amazed that vast companies like JC Penney, with the top American manufacturers jostling for orders, had asked me to design for them and I'd just said, 'OK, what do we do?' The amazing thing about being young is that yes, you're scared, but you take it for granted that you can do it. And so I did, with both fashion and make-up. Europe joined in and Japan followed.

# The Pill

FASHION WAS STIMULATED enormously by the arrival of 'the Pill'– the atomic bomb of human relationships, and possible saviour of the planet – but you could not have it, not on the National Health, nor privately, unless you had certain other specifications and needs. We also believed that the Pill was going to give us cancer.

So there it was, but you could not have it.

I went to my local Chelsea GP who said no – and suggested instead the charming 'Dutch Cap', instead of the alternative, the 'French Letter'. He explained to me how you coated this springy thing with a gel, which I was warned was poisonous. This had to be applied every time. When I looked sceptical and unenthused, he qualified things by saying, 'No, it's simple. You just pop this in when you change for dinner.'

It had not occurred to me that copulation took place at dinner parties.

And it had not occurred to me that you had to change for dinner.

# The Wet Collection

ONE DAY A new fabric appeared on the scene. It was new, it was shiny, it was black and white and like nothing one had ever seen before. And it was waterproof. It was called PVC. I was stunned. I loved the black and white but also persuaded the manufacturers to make me some in a ginger, terracotta colour and a Colman's mustard yellow as well.

I designed big batwing tunics, belted trench coats, sou'westers and back-buttoning smocks. We made them in our studio, on the same machines as the rest of the dresses and clothes collections. The first horror was discovering that the seams would tear like perforated stamps but some special thread and machine needles were made for us and we solved the problem.

The whole look worked. I called it, appropriately enough, the Wet Collection.

Jon Bannenberg, a yacht designer and friend, begged me to convert the small conservatory in our Chelsea ballroom flat into a PVC-covered black-and-white extravaganza, with silver Venetian blinds over the windows. The effect was overwhelming. It seemed to have a similar impact on Snowdon, who wanted to photograph me in one of the PVC raincoats in the PVC room. The photographs are dynamic and fun but caused a lot of bother because Princess Margaret thought it was just an excuse for an affair between us and telephoned every five minutes. I know Snowdon was one of the best flirts in London but we were focusing only on the pictures. It was a Sunday and Alexander sensibly went to the Classic Cinema for the duration of the shoot. It rained. The pictures were great.

This was the part of the collection that won us the *Sunday Times* International Fashion Award. We showed it in Paris for the first time in 1963. No one had seen the stuff before so when the fourteen-year-old daughter of journalist Dee Wells, Gully, came pounding down the catwalk in the batwing mini-length tunic − all long legs and youthful exuberance − it had huge impact.

Incidentally, being an old friend, when Snowdon married Princess Margaret in 1960 we were invited to the wedding. Press-wise, all hell broke loose − headlines like 'Shopkeepers Invited to Royal Wedding' screamed from the pages. We were besieged in our flat for days. APG decided on a wonderfully apt wedding present of duelling pistols. We had great trouble having these delivered to Buckingham Palace since the palace had to produce special gun licences for us, but they arrived on time, and in good order.

# Knickers

THE FIRST UNDERWEAR design project put to us was a seriously large proposition. The chairman of the company was an important politician, Kenneth Baker. I still like to tease him that we were in knickers together.

To concentrate on the designs for a tight deadline, Alexander and I took ten days away in Connemara, Ireland. Now Connemara is a heavenly place with exquisite racehorses standing about near the seashore like ghostly Elisabeth Frink sculptures, plus the odd grumpy donkey, and very few people or houses. So we were thought strange and suspicious visitors to be there, before the fishing season, in spite of the Irish surname Plunket Greene. The staff of the nearly empty hotel, seeing my underwear sketches laid out on the floor, decided it must be pornography, and we could not be married. We had been married for some time by then, but they put a card on the dinner table reserved for us, in the almost-deserted dining room, that said 'Plunket Greene and party' – the party being me, which somehow was a flattering label to have.

Every afternoon we walked and swam in that delicate Irish

drizzle. I loved it. We would return back to work in our hire car to find it licked to death. We had been feeding sugar-lumps and apples to the horses, who decided we were made of sugar. We would drive back as in intense fog, with the windows coated with expectant juices.

This Mary Quant underwear collection led to some gutsy photographs and started the idea of underwear as outerwear. It also led me on to working on much softer ideas, which were manufactured for me by Swaren Curry of the Nylon Hosiery Company Ltd, made on knit machines, and the vast development of our tights and pantyhose. After that I could persuade the giant fashion retailer JC Penney to produce both in America. I am to be credited for America discovering pantyhose, or I am to be blamed for it, depending on which way you look at it.

# On Creating an Icon

WHEN DRAWING EARLY roughs for the clothes I'd doodle on the designs as I was working – I used to doodle all the time – and I'd often think, 'Something needs to go here or there.' I knew I needed a focal point so while I was working out the shape and so on, I would doodle this daisy. I'd put it on the design and it made it look happy; it just worked. It was always better than anything else.

To begin with the daisy varied quite a bit. It might have five petals or it might have six petals and sometimes it would be one way up and sometimes another! Later, when we began the cosmetics, the daisy had to be regularised so it could be trademarked. We agreed on five petals with the circle in the centre. It wasn't until then that it was always the same.

Once I had the daisy, I stuck with it. I used it on mini-skirts, belts, tunic dresses, and underwear. It worked terribly well.

Right from the beginning the daisy was very lucky for me. I love the way it reads so well from a distance, a greater distance than any other logo perhaps except the Mercedes sign. Girls can flash the make-up at each other as a sign of camaraderie. At the same time the daisy implies a freshness and vulnerability laced with sexy chic.

Chanel was right. For beauty, white camellias rip one's heart, but they do not have the optimism and gaiety of my daisy.

# The Ginger Group

THE GINGER GROUP was to be a young provocative collection manufactured by the best women's clothing manufacturers, Butte Knit and Alexon, produced by Steinberg & Sons in South Wales. The idea was that it would be a lower-priced line designed to appeal to a wider market. It was very often the fabrics that excited me and gave me the key to a collection. But with the new Ginger Group collection, launched in 1963, I visualised the clothes and look I wanted first, and then designed the fabrics to achieve them.

Colour was essential to my new vision. I have always studied the colour forcasting that goes on at the fabric trade fares such as Première Vision, Frankfurt and Como. I would digest the trends and then, seeing the new palette as a background for mine, I would think, 'What colours would look jumpingly different or coolly sane, by contrast?' Store windows will be awash with the forecasted colour range and people will feel sick of it before they even start buying because collections go into the stores so early. So if the hot colours are pastels, one feels pale and washed out early in spring, and if it is something strong like rhubarb pink or screaming lime, one thinks,

'Thank God for black and white and navy, or even a cold dead brown.' Another season I long for a 'help!' colour like screaming orange, or a bleached-out pinkish clay colour. But I always return to black: blue-black, bad dusky black, liquorice black, just any way black. And why leave out white, whether it's dazzling white, a chalky white ecru or string?

For the Ginger Group I naturally wanted a hot ginger colour, as well as Colman's mustard yellow, a smart grapey-prune colour, putty and black. They were all unfashionable colours then. I needed plain fabric and a bold stripe – ginger and black, putty and black etc. – all in wool jersey with a lightly bonded back to hold the form. The next step was to have skinny ribbed sweaters developed, to be worn with the tunic dresses and mini-skirts. Next I would need some crêpe and crêpe de Chine shirts and blouses, as well as tights, boots and over-the-knee socks in most of the colours. This worked well too, but all the fabrics had to be made especially for us. We had to start providing quantity forecasts, which is always a hell of a gamble. You can get it wrong simply by being so damn right.

Collections depend on so many things to be a success or otherwise. First of all you need to liaise expertly between the designers, tailors, pattern cutters, sample machinists and manufacturers. Then you are reliant on the seduction of marketing, the skill of models, the expertise of the make-up artists, the buzz of the catwalk, the talent of photographers, the interest of fashion editors and the available space in magazines. Then there is the power of the brand, the packaging, the advertising and the timing. And after all that you need a sympathetic and chic sales girl. Throw into the mix the hats, shoes, boots, bags, belts, beads and Vidal Sassoon – and stand well back to see if your new collection catches fire or not.

The strength of Steinberg/Alexon/Butte Knit's reputation made it possible to persuade the fabric manufacturers to make what I wanted in large quantities so that I could produce the coordinating collection. We persuaded Swaren Curry to work with us on the tights as he was prepared to invest in pantyhose machinery. Until this time I had only managed to persuade theatre manufacturers to make tights, as no stocking producers had the machines to make them. Only Italy seemed able to produce some very classy textured tights, though they were often expensive and marketed only for countrywear, shooting and so on. Alexander was enchanted by Swaren Curry's name, because he was Indian. After our original success I then persuaded Swaren to make pants and socks and to knit bra tops in the same flexible knit. I did drawings and asked men's knitwear manufacturers to make their men's cardigans longer and make cricket sweaters mini-skirt length for women, in Colman's-mustard yellow, black, white and ginger. Swaren Curry matched the colours of the opaque tights to the sweaters for me.

Alexander produced some wonderful names, such as Pop Sox for the striped socks and Brighton Rock Socks. The timely arrival of these in the stores was perfect. The bras and pants were comfortable to wear and they did not distort the natural body shape, providing only minimum, gentle control. This gave us the 'No-Bra' effect that was becoming so desired at the time, as popularised by Rudi Gernreich.

The most successful dresses were tunic-shaped. They had sleeveless, plain V-necked top halves and drop-waisted striped skirts, giving a two-piece effect. The tops were laced up across the very

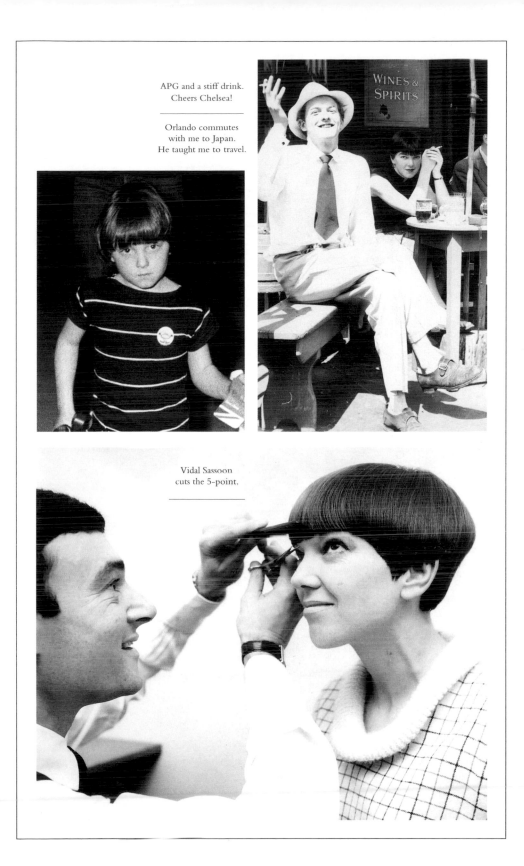

APG and a stiff drink.
Cheers Chelsea!

Orlando commutes
with me to Japan.
He taught me to travel.

Vidal Sassoon
cuts the 5-point.

Antony Rouse:
prototype for cricketer
Stuart Broad. He too
would drop in.

Taking to country life
in Surrey with
Orlando, APG and
Blossom the dog.

With APG in the
Ball Room flat at
the Nunnery Table.

OPG has a Coke.

**BRING BACK THE LASH!**

What a brilliantly sensible
way to buy eyelashes

**MARY QUANT** ✿

Jean Shrimpton
in the "Daddy's Girl"
MQ dress.
Winning girl;
bestselling dress.

Tom Wolsey designed
the huge posters
for the "Bring Back
the Lash" campaign.
False eyelashes cut
by the yard.

low V-neck and worn over a skinny rib sweater, and the skirt part would be inserted with godets (extra panels that caused it to flare). We used contrasting-coloured jeans-style stitching throughout the collection. We also produced mini-skirts in the same fabrics and knits or crêpe shirts in the same groups of colours. I later produced shirt-dresses in crêpe with the same sporty, jeans-style contrast stitching, complete with a multi-stitched tie belt such as only raincoats ever had.

These dresses became a classic, and still are to this day, especially in black crêpe stitched with white thread, or brown crêpe stitched with white. The sporty look of the crêpe was completely new. I exaggerated it by always using men's sexy trouser buttons throughout the Ginger Group collections.

Because Steinberg had the power to persuade textile manufacturers to produce these new fabrics in my colours and design in such quantities, it allowed me to, or even made me, make the entire collection very cohesive, which added to its powerful effect.

I showed the collection with leather caps (Lennon bought one), berets and sou'wester hats made of the same jersey fabric and colour. The shoes were high vamp and slingback with a lowish heel, made for me by Ballet. The whole collection had a feeling of rightful inevitability, which was part of its strength and charm. I have never known a collection that seemed to come together like clockwork in such a pleasing way. This was the collection, along with the famous Wet Collection, which won us the *Sunday Times* International Fashion award in 1964, voted for by the top fashion press in France and America. It was shown in Paris along with the other international couture winners.

Chanel, one of the other winners, ducked out of the ceremony as she hated me, the gossips said, despite me being a major fan of hers.

# What's in a Name?

I TEND TO be asked the same questions by students and people generally so it was a surprise to be asked the toughest question only once and by a fellow designer, too. It was: 'How much did your name and Terence Conran's name help, do you think?' I had never thought of it like that, but I certainly have since. My answer was — quite a lot, I think.

Not only does Mary Quant have a visual pattern to it but also a rhythm. The 'Q' is particularly strong and jumps out of the page or across a street, but it is also female and pleasing. The 'M' is a dominant graphic letter and the 'Y' is soothing. I don't think I could have been called anything else.

I agree that Terence Conran is a particularly satisfying name as well. The designer was right. In return I asked him whether that was why he worked for Conran.

My favourite name is that of a professional golfer. I know nothing about golf, except the shape of those bunkers, which visually offend me — but this man's name is great. It's Fred Funk and I can never forget it. It's ugly, strong, pleasing, masculine and totally satisfactory.

Alexander was good at inventing names that were always dashing or amusing. One of my favourites was for our foundation: Starkers. There was a waterproof mascara called Cry Baby, bras were called Booby Traps and tights were Bacon Savers. Why? Because they saved your bacon! Alexander was a brilliant natural marketing man who made Mary Quant the success it is.

# Puritan Fashions

IN 1965 WE spent the weekend with Carl Rosen, the millionaire owner of the large American ready-to-wear chain, Puritan Fashions, for whom we had been asked to create some exclusive designs. We stayed at his house — or at least in various guesthouses on his property. These annexes were equipped with fully stocked bars and stocked with snacks, nuts and chocolate. We did not realise that these constituted our meals and became so hungry we ate the green tomatoes ripening round the pool. On Saturday night we were taken to a Chinese restaurant, but Carl was overwhelmed by the problems of ordering and suddenly became infuriated, leaving the restaurant and insisting we all troop out behind him. Being British, we did not realise that if you were hungry you should go to the kitchen door of the main house and the staff would cook you anything you wanted.

When progressing further into the main house you were directed to take off your shoes. The carpets were already covered with plastic wrapping and were so dense they were like box hedging, making a sort of Versailles-style indoor garden maze that was difficult not to trip over.

On Sunday it was decided we all should go for a swim. This meant going by car to the local airport, collecting Carl's aeroplane and pilot and flying to the sea. I said I longed to learn to fly so I was promptly allowed to take the dual controls, directed by the pilot. This absolutely thrilled me but wasn't so great for APG and our friends Sandie Moss, Chester Jones and Paul Young, by now all working for Carl, who were sitting in the tail and threw up. It was thought wise that they returned by limousine while Carl, the pilot and I had a further flying lesson on the way back to New York, the pilot virtually allowing me to land under his dire directions coupled with too much champagne. For me this was a thrilling introduction to American life, and for Carl it was a way of interrogating me as to who was sleeping with whom, as many friends of ours were on his payroll and had been whisked off to the States to help develop his new store in New York. My English reserve came to my defence.

Bulletproof cars and enormously powerful fashion buyers who were parachuted into stores by the manufacturers were further introductions to the American way of doing things. Becoming rather nervous about this mafia way of life, APG, Archie McNair and I started to rue the day that we had given up our contract with JC Penney to work with Puritan Inc. Back in London, after a late lunch worrying about this problem, we decided to ask Carl Rosen to let us go on working for JC Penney so that I could design a collection for both Penney *and* Puritan Inc. We decided that the only way to do this was to split the royalties from Penney's with Carl. I was persuaded there and then to catch the last flight out to New York and put it to him.

So late was this flight that I was the only passenger in first class.

In those days caviar was the treat of treats when flying and I knew that the cabin would have that large dinnerplate-sized tin of caviar – once opened never to be abandoned – so I persuaded the steward to forget dinner, saying that instead he and I should have the caviar and champagne. This ended up being the most luxurious flight to New York as I was given the pilot's bed on board to sleep in, as well as being allowed up into the cabin for landing, which was an enormous thrill for me.

Next day I caught Carl in his office just before lunch and tried to persuade him to let me go on designing for JC Penney, offering him the entire proceeds of the royalties in return. Carl was so bowled over by this suggestion that he burst into tears, saying nobody had ever given him anything for nothing in all his life. I quickly suggested that, well then, perhaps fifty-fifty would do it. In response, Carl pulled an enormous bunch of keys from his desk, saying, 'Here are the keys of my business: they are yours if you will come to Miami with me this weekend.'

Stunned by this equally generous offer, I retreated and insisted he purely give me the rights to split the royalties with him and that he telephone his lawyer and mine right away to finalise the deal. This was done, but the lawyers said it had to be signed by both me and the lawyers that afternoon as it was a Friday and I had to fly back the next day. Carl produced a bottle of champagne to celebrate but I just grabbed the Krug, blew him a kiss and swept out on to Fifth Avenue with it. I had to get to the lawyers before 4.30 p.m. as they had insisted.

In New York that day there was a transport strike, so there was not a free cab in town. I walked straight out into the traffic, holding the bottle of champagne aloft, in front of a passing driver who had to kill me or stop. 'This is for you if you will get me to my lawyers before 4.30,' I said. The driver, surprised by my ambush, thinking perhaps divorce or a legacy, got caught up in my hysteria and drove me at breakneck speed to the office, making it by 4.25. It was like being in the movies. All was signed and I had a celebratory dinner that night with the lawyers.

But with the extra design work we were now doing up to eighteen collections a year, as Ernestine Carter had been quietly calculating for her famous article.

# Bones

I HAVE ALWAYS wanted to write a sort of love letter to supermodels, or perhaps more accurately to their bones. It is not a matter of simply being thin, as fat people tend to think. It is about having really clear-cut bones jutting out in the right place, at the right angle, as well as long legs and beauty. Clothes need to hang in the right way from the shoulder and hip-bones particularly, and a long thigh is great, as 1930s fashion shows, so starving yourself near to death is not going to do the trick. Sophie Dahl looked great when she was both fat and thin. Stella Tennant was said by her grandmother to be a great loss to the lambing season when she started modelling so successfully, but she was a wonder to the fashion trade. Kate Moss, the most successful model ever, is relatively small, but the bones of her face and body do all the right things, as Lucian Freud spotted when he painted her pregnant. Lily Cole the wonder model has a doll-like face, but quite a strong body frame – no anorexic nonsense there. She is much too bright and does not need to starve.

It's the bones, the beauty, and the deep appetite for and appreciation of fashion, style and design that makes a model truly great.

The most beautiful of all the models I have known was Jean Shrimpton. To walk down the King's Road, Chelsea, with Shrimpton was like walking through the rye. Strong men just keeled over right and left as she strode up the street. I remember Bailey telling me it was a strain photographing actresses and film stars after the Shrimp, because they could not touch her for beauty. Shrimpton herself seemed to have no awareness of her extraordinary looks.

Jean's minders once asked Alexander if we would develop a further collection in her name, which was an attractive idea, but I was already designing eighteen collections a year at the time and becoming pretty exhausted. A Shrimpton collection would need to have a completely unique Shrimpton point of view and style, plus accompanying packaging and branding. I saw this to be a classical English country look, brought up to date. However, I was already using country knickerbockers, shooting jackets and horse blankets as inspiration for my other collections, so I said no, with both relief and regret because I liked her.

But Alexander had the fun of thinking he owned the Shrimp for five whole days.

# Extruded Moulded Shoe-Boots

PRODUCING EXTRUDED MOULDED shoe-boots sounded like an exciting possibility. I imagined Cinderella-like clear glass slippers, foot-shaped boots and all-in-one pantyhose or tights and flip-flops.

The Kingswood-based work-boot manufacturers GB Brittan were game to try all these ideas, which made things fun – but 'first offs' also cause problems. We know now that plastic is never crystal clear and plastic boots are sweaty. We should have realised we could throw them in the washing machine, but washing machines were so sacred and new at that time that no one would do that. (Though on my trip to India, I discovered that in the countryside there, you made butter or ghee in the spin dryer.)

Of the boots we made in the mid-sixties, I like the long vamped mule boot best, which still has a great look. These days we would throw it in the washing machine without a backward glance.

# Italian Fame

I HAD WON a very important fashion award in Italy in 1966 and the award ceremony would take place in Rome, firstly outdoors on the Spanish Steps and then in a grand store, with my collection being shown there. We arrived in Rome on a blissfully perfect sun-baked spring day and were then told we could not go on to the helicopter and land on the steps because the bad weather made it too dangerous.

There was uproar in the airport where hundreds of students had arrived to welcome me and were furious at the Spanish Steps ceremony being cancelled, as the bad weather excuse was so obviously not true. Riots started to break out. The helicopter was there waiting with the pilot, so seeing the trouble brewing the authorities had a change of heart and we were allowed to get in, landing on the Spanish Steps as promised. We were mobbed but went into the smart department store where my collection was to be shown, where we were met by an even larger crowd chanting, 'Ave Maria!' Rome loved the mini-skirt – after all, Rome loved legs and that day they sure loved Mary too.

My huge limousine was rocked when we tried to leave, with the students still chanting 'Ave Maria' and trying to grab bits of me as a souvenir. I have never been more frightened. Thank goodness we had three or four huge store managers there to protect us, but I was still utterly terrified. I could not sleep all that summer as I started suffering from nightmares about being torn apart. Fame has its ups and downs but three-monthly visits to my analyst sorted that one.

Fame and celebrity are very hard to handle. I was once accosted by a very unpleasant man in Canada late at night when I arrived at our hotel after a long, long delayed flight. Some journalists were waiting for me there. One of them, a man, said to me: 'You're not very charismatic, are you?' To which I replied, rather bad-temperedly: 'No, I haven't bothered to switch on yet just for you. Give me a glass of wine and I will try.'

On some PR launch trips I had to do in Europe and USA, one journalist would be employed to photograph me every minute of the day whatever the rest of the pack did. This was bitterly exhausting. If you so much as lit a cigarette or drank some wine you knew the attention would be intensified. By the end of the day I would try to make friends with the photographer and negotiate a truce because you do start to feel so crazy and exhausted. The PR agency would then give me a book of the resulting endless photos afterwards, which you had to thank them for.

I see how one can follow the route to drug-taking only too easily if you are in this position. But it is almost impossible to water down drugs or control their effects safely. It may be rather thin by comparison but I find that good wine is much the simplest mood-changer to handle and it can prolong your tolerance almost indefinitely, which is what you need. A good, not too strong, white wine like Sancerre is much the best. (Red wine can be spilt down your front, the only remedy for which is to pour a whole bottle of white wine on top of it. An air steward taught me this once when it happened to me during a flight to Australia. It was amazingly satisfying and worked well, despite the fact I was wearing a terrific white dress and pants – it was refreshing too but a rather expensive solution, I suppose. I was arriving to a press welcome in Australia and the English rugby team were on the same flight, so they carried me off the plane in honour, soaking wet, across the tarmac.)

Enjoy the fame and never forget your good fortune. The viciousness of envy is inevitable, so enjoy the good bits of fame, of which there are so many. Strangers smiling at you in friendly recognition is lovely. Celebrity is delicious, there is no doubt – if you can stay in control of it. The ideal situation is to be able to turn it on and turn it off at will, but of course this is mighty difficult.

# OBE

FRANKFURT WAS ALWAYS the toughest fabric-buying fair. I had to go twice every year. I had also been working in Paris with the French perfume companies to develop our new product, Mary Quant Perfume. Arriving back in London, Alexander appeared before customs in the airport. Somehow he had got permission to go through and he rushed me back out, saying, 'Something marvellous has happened – you've got the OBE!' This was 1966, the same year as the Beatles and pop broke down new barriers. British fashion had never achieved such honours before so the press in London was ecstatic.

I admit it was very exciting. Archie, Alexander and I went to the palace and my parents came too. The Queen was charming and the Guards Band played the 'Teddy Bears' Picnic' in our honour.

Harold Pinter was gonged on the same day and he and I got lost out of sheer terror in those long corridors at Buckingham Palace. He admitted being as scared as I was, which surprised me.

On my next New York trip my award was celebrated in a very smart restaurant. Suddenly they pointed spotlights onto me and declared, 'Here is Mary Quant, recently knighted by the Queen!' After I had been knighted, they then trained the spotlight on Alexander. There was a long pause before the announcement came: 'Alexander Plunket Greene – Englishman!', which was stated gloriously, with huge importance.

# The Hipster Pants Disaster

ALEXANDER'S FATHER WAS an incredibly attractive and dashing man – a right charmer and womaniser – and no one could resist him. His suits were cut and made in New York, to achieve the hipster cowboy look he demanded. Alexander adopted the same style himself, and I soon learnt to have my pants made by his tailors – Dougie Hayward – in Savile Row, who copied this style. I used to go on a bus week after week to fitting after fitting to get the pants just the right degree of hipster and fit, known in the tailoring trade as Cavalry overalls in Cavalry twill. The final fit was so good that they were rather over-gratifying to wear. But this was research for both me and for the Savile Row tailors, as they had never made pants for women before.

I had long wanted to produce the best-cut pants in the world and to make this the basis of the coordinating pieces in the Ginger Group collection. Since my idea of the best pants followed the hipster cut of Alexander and his father, I felt the way to do this was to work with an American manufacturer and make pants using jeans-style block patterns, in whatever the fabric was that season. This meant going to America because only denim was cut in this way there. So when an American jeans sportswear manufacturer actually approached us to work with him, I was delighted and turned down a British approach from an expert skirt manufacturer. I believed that America and some French firms cut the best pants in the world. As you can only somewhat modify a manufacturer's block patterns and approach, this was good sense.

We decided the first drawings and samples should be created in London. The production counter samples were made in the USA and fine-tuned and passed finally back in London. I wanted the jackets, pants and skirts to be made in very English-looking classic fabrics of flannel, corduroy and heavy crêpe, in pale grey, ochre/chestnut and black. Shirts and tops were to be lightweight crêpe and brushed cotton.

The samples came through superbly. No one then had put such fabrics into jeans factories. These were shown to the press and buyers in a mock-up of how they would look in a shop with all their coordinated variations plus accessories. This was a prodigious success, such ideas being utterly new at that time. The buyers loved it and ordered enormous quantities for their stores around the country. We had to decide which store groups and which specialised boutiques would be allowed the collection, as there was such a demand. So successful was the launch that some of the more friendly and affectionate press said, 'You've really hit the jackpot and achieved the perfect formula with this collection idea.'

We also showed in Paris at the prêt-à-porter collections with great success; the samples and sizing were just right. Americans do know sizing and have finessed their sizing classifications so that you can risk buying in America without trying clothes on, if you know your size and type – Junior, Miss, Missie etc. If you can accept these silly words for the classifications and stay in your size without getting fatter, clothes will look made to measure. This is why American pants hang so well on your bone structure. The French achieve this by knowing precisely the type of women they are designing for and in turn you quickly learn which is the right-sized brand for you. By contrast, British manufacturers never seem to agree what a size eight or ten or twelve is, or even whether they are using French or Italian sizing.

Our American backer and manufacturer in this enterprise had been very keen and insisted we took on as head of sales an American salesman from his favourite store on the west coast of California. This recently married young man had been through Vietnam and had suffered something close to a breakdown afterwards, running away to South America. His mother had gone out to Mexico and found him and talked him back. He and his wife moved to England. A young woman from his manufacturing company also moved to London to organise the planning and delivery of stock.

There was the usual proof of a good collection, with samples being stolen and a punch-up at the warehouse. But come the delivery dates nothing happened. Nothing arrived – nothing. The stores were justifiably furious. A large part of their buying quota had been applied to this collection. All hell broke loose. The collection had been photographed everywhere in the magazines and daily papers, so the press were angry too. Further horrors emerged. The American samples were found to be stuffed with drugs within the seams. Many people disappeared and were never seen again.

Suddenly the plugs were pulled on all the machines in the American company. Legal proceedings started in the USA against the manufacturer. When I asked the owner why he had not told us about the problems, he said his daughter was getting married that summer and he had just wanted to avoid the embarrassment until after the wedding.

My own embarrassment and disappointment is still ripe.

# Cosmetics

I WANTED TO design a complete look from head to toe. We had the mini-skirt and mini-dresses. We had the tights to match the skinny-rib sweaters, in great colours like Colman's mustard yellow, plum, ginger and black. We had Vidal Sassoon.

Everything looked right except the make-up.

Cosmetics had become stuck. Before we came along they were about as fashionable and chic as false teeth, the preserve of middle age. The companies that made them were huge and international and saw no reason to change with fashion. They were complacent. Most were American, with the cosmetics devised for the needs of Hollywood. They saw lipstick as only ever being red, pink or orange and the same went for nail polish. The look was hard and lacquered, à la Joan Crawford, and sold by dragon-like ladies who frightened people away. Eye shadow had to be blue, green or purple. I don't think they even did brown. Cosmetic packaging was always pink, gold and kidney-shaped.

Not surprisingly, many people, especially men, disapproved of cosmetics – they thought them vulgar and only to be worn by film stars or whores. Other women used cosmetics very surreptitiously; it was not meant to show and was only put on in the bathroom. Applying cosmetics in public was somehow taboo. It was like a woman sitting alone on a high stool at the bar, ordering a drink – just not done. In fact if you did that, you would be asked to go and sit at a table and wait for a waiter. As a career woman, sometimes travelling alone internationally, I found this offensive, and felt much better placed sitting at a bar talking to the barman when wanting a drink of wine on my own. It seemed less inviting of company than sitting alone at a table, and had the added protection of proximity to the barman.

So regarding cosmetics, I was acutely conscious that I had to deliberately break the rules. As an art student I'd been using my Caran d'Ache crayons and watercolour brushes to do my make-up, merging the colours as I pleased. You could achieve a very natural look so that no one realised you were wearing make-up at all. I found you could also be very extreme by using the fashion colours of your clothes to achieve surreal effects. Then I saw Jean Shrimpton and Grace Coddington using foot-long brushes from stage make-up suppliers. This moved my thinking further. I could see that these could be developed into a pencil-case size and made very chic and charming. A wider palette of subtle foundation and blusher colours would also give us the shading, shaping and shadowing effects needed to flatter the face. These could still be cigarette-case-size palettes, with brushes or sponge applicators, so they would be small, elegant and irresistible. I wanted to develop a collection of make-up that used different colours, different textures and different ways of application – and all in make-up boxes that you could carry around in your handbag. I wanted to change cosmetics into make-up.

Make-up is fun.

Make-up is play.

Make-up is dreams.

Make-up is illusion.

Make-up makes you beautiful.

Make-up is making love to yourself.

Make-up is putting yourself in the mood for love.

The make-up I wanted needed to be flattering, exaggerating the eyes, the cheekbones and mouth, subtly shaping the face, very pale in winter or playing up freckles in summer. I love the 'nude' face, with bleached eyebrows, palest foundation and luminous pale pink lip colours. I also enjoy seeing a pale face with exaggerated dark eyebrows. I love the ability we now all have to play with make-up, and to change and enjoy ourselves.

I wanted Mary Quant cosmetic packaging to be beautiful too, chic like cigarette lighters or some mobiles now, and flourished in the smartest bars and restaurants. After it was launched, girls did just that. The Mary Quant lipstick became a symbol of the new, young career woman and they flashed it across restaurants at each other. It was like being a member of a club.

I talked with several cosmetic manufacturers who got very excited but they were only interested in doing a single-season promotion. Then a marvellous American cosmetic manufacturer, Stanley Picker, an Anglophile to his toes, came into our garage studio and told me he would show me how to do it technically. He was a Russian Jew living in America and had been a cosmetic man all his life. He could see that I was trying to do something completely different that had never been done before. We got so excited we started work that afternoon and carried on half the night, along with his PA, discussing how and why and what we would do. The packaging was to be black and white and silver and the product would be pure colour. It was the most exciting day of my life.

We spent eighteen months developing the Mary Quant cosmetic brand before it launched. The developing, packaging, testing and launching was the most thrilling time for me. I had no doubts at all about my concept of the colours and products, as to me the need of the new was so glaringly obvious, but when the packaging and testing also went so smoothly and looked so terrific, it was the one time in my life I had total, total confidence in a venture's success. Stanley Picker simply let me rip from an ideas point of view, which I had never experienced before, and during the tests with his team and skills everything came out right. There was a tide to it all.

I had a very handsome Gladstone bag I carried about with me before the launch, containing all the major products in their final packaging and ready to go. I could not stop showing them to friends, colleagues and strangers in the street or garages or wherever I went, I was so chuffed with it. APG had come up with some wonderfully apt names. So there was Starkers foundation, Blush Baby blusher, Jeepers Peepers eyeshadow and Bring Back the Lash mascara, replacing all those bogus French names, sold by middle-aged harridans. Mary Quant cosmetics were going to be sold by girls in mini-skirts, looking like top models, or by dashing young men in jeans. It's probably hard to imagine the impact now because it established the way forward, but I can never forget my pleasure in the way my new make-up looked.

Breaking rules is so revitalising. Not only did I want to re-invent make-up colours and packaging, but I knew I had to develop a waterproof mascara too. Mascara then had to have a huge fat scrubbing brush to apply it. Spit and scrub was the traditional technique. Like most women I loved to swim and I loved to go to the movies, but if the water was wet and the film was a weepy, my mascara ended up smeared and smudged all round my face. I had a hard time in persuading the laboratory and the chemists and manufacturers as to why making waterproof mascara was important. They just didn't see the need. They said, 'Why do you want it? Women swim with their heads out of the water.' Of course I replied, 'That's because of their make-up!' I got them to start work and together we did it.

We tested its waterproofing ability when I was on holiday in the South of France. I was so surprised to find these very chic French women following me into the changing rooms of swimming pools and saying, 'What is that mascara you are wearing? It stays on!' Then I realised we had a success – a real success. The trouble was it was so waterproof it was very hard to take off. When it was first launched, girls used to boast about how many days they could keep it on! So we had to modify it and we developed a special solvent. Cry Baby mascara with Lift Off remover. Sensational.

The Mary Quant cosmetic advertisements had a wildly daring approach devised by Tom Wolsey. Tom was the art director on *Man About Town*, the magazine that was electrifying London right then. Long evenings were spent with him discussing our approach. We agreed on the products to promote – we would focus on the most original and provocative at the time: the waterproof mascara, false eyelashes and eyeshadow colours. Now we had to come up with an advertising strategy.

No one had used a face on billboards, blown up to twice the size of any seen before, to sell cosmetics. Vast blow-ups of Shadow Boxing appeared in South Kensington underground station – on the wrong side of the track, so you had to look at it while waiting on the platform. Huge adverts featuring Cry Baby and Bring Back the Lash were pasted in the King's Road, Chelsea. Driving down there one Monday morning I was blinded by my first sighting of the Cry Baby billboard and crashed my black Mini Minor. These adverts had the classic sixties Pop Art look of Joe Tilson and Tom Wesselman. Pop Art itself was playing with scale and billboard-size images. And we were playing with it back in the grossly enlarged dimensions of street advertising.

It was so popular that fans would photograph the photographs.

Mary Quant Cosmetics was launched in 1966. People were stunned by the look of the whole brand. The packaging was terrific and the products completely new. They were amazed by the white gloss-like Vaseline effect of the make-up and the extraordinary colours: the bois de rose and luminous pinks, the mustard yellows, oranges, scarlets, sepias and matt whites. I had brought fashion colours into cosmetics, emphasising how beautiful fingertips could be a part of one's dress, rather than inevitably matching the colour of one's lipstick. This surprised and delighted everyone and took off straight away. It was the most frightening success, particularly in Japan. Because Japanese children first learn to write with a brush, they are immensely skilled and dexterous in applying make-up. As soon as my Japanese partners started to manufacture the make-up, I knew the quality and finesse would be terrific. The tradition of quality and skill in Nakayama's company goes back three generations and produces exquisite cosmetics. Young women in Japan love Mary Quant make-up and love fashion.

Back home, Kevin Roberts, here from New Zealand and just into long pants (he's now the worldwide CEO of Saatchi & Saatchi), recruited a team of dashing young men and girls who were models. He took them through Europe in a bus, parking in the centre of major cities at lunchtimes. Out came all these pretty mini-skirted girls and jeans-clad boys to show you how to use Mary Quant make-up. Brussels, Madrid, Paris, Milan: the girls flocked from all over the continent. It was younger, more natural and softer than anything that had gone before – and the style of our selling was in sharp contrast to the staid tradition of cosmetics being sold by awe-inspiring middle-aged ladies stood behind counters.

The whole launch of Mary Quant make-up had a huge impact. It was soon stocked all over the world. One time, I was going out to Sweden to launch our cosmetics and they sent a helicopter to our house in the country here, which was a new and thrilling experience. Everyone loved the new range. The idea of the stark black, white and silver presentation, making the colour of the products the focus, led me to persuade our shops to look more like art shops with banks of colour where customers were encouraged to experiment. The demonstrators showed people how to do their make-up to great effect. Out went those dowager saleswomen. This led to the idea of employing young men to do 'makeovers' for customers, and devise an individually drawn colour 'recipe' for young women to take away with them. It changed the way make-up was sold and presented, and sent the waterproof mascara's specification worldwide. I can see in retrospect that I changed cosmetics into make-up. And make-up *is* fashion and fun. Lipstick in 101 colours!

The travelling became so intense it was quite hard to get the design work and collections done. But I loved it all and thrived. The 'house wear', or 'leisure wear' as it was called in the USA, was also selling like mad. I had enjoyed designing this project very much and it showed. Much of this was made in Sweden so we visited the west coast of the country where the Swedish people more or less bagged their own island and used helicopters all the time. Wonderful fish would be washed down with aquavit for lunch and dinner. The Swedes seemed to dine near midnight so given the huge quantities of aquavit consumed they would get very drunk and make prodigious speeches and skåls! It must be down to the long dark winters. One top female journalist at a business dinner was carried out like a plank, and no one seemed in the least embarrassed.

The only problems with Mary Quant Cosmetics came from its colossal success. It changed the way all other manufacturers developed cosmetics and it became the new starting point for all other brands. This was consolidated by my second make-up brand idea, Special Recipes, launched in the early seventies. This I saw as the development of a natural, subtle, organic approach to make-up and it, too, was very successful.

But I did not anticipate the drastic effects of industry rivalry. The worst being that after the trials and tribulations of the Three-Day Week recession, while a new, bigger factory was being built alongside the old factory on the Surbiton bypass and the Quant daisy flag was flying on a flagpole outside, Stanley Picker was forced to sell part of his company to Max Factor. Production slowed and in some cases stopped. No waterproof black mascara was being made. Stanley was mortified and went off to Russia to explore his roots. Looking back, it seems to me Max Factor rather neglected Mary Quant Cosmetics, expending energy on its own brands instead. They produced only a small trayful of products to be developed and tested. If something was good, it seemed they would take it straight to the other Max Factor brands. While understandable in the economic circumstances of the enormous recession, it was a problem for everyone working on Mary Quant Cosmetics.

American managers and salesmen were sent to London and lived the life of colonial toffs – riding in Richmond Park in the morning, lunching at Wheeler's, going to museums in the afternoon and the theatre in the evening. They were very generous and charming to me and invited me along but I could see it was a disaster for my cosmetics brand. Some of the Max Factor top executives were as keen as I was to go on developing Mary Quant Cosmetics and there were plenty of ideas, but it was not to be. Ronald Perelman of Revlon bought out all Max Factor's portfolio of brands, and that was that.

But the Japanese went on manufacturing and selling the cosmetics – and do so to this day in about 200 outlets.

# Vitamins

IT'S HARD TO believe now but I caused innocent outrage by launching vitamin pills to go with the Mary Quant make-up and skincare. They were the result of my mother's sensible lectures on eating well and going to bed early to give glowing skin instead of simply using make-up to cover up a lifeless complexion.

The pills were vitamins B and D, and were sold in classic pillboxes with the Mary Quant logo on it. They were stocked next to the skincare range. They were a great add-on, and received tons of attention. Chemists were furious, as they saw themselves as doctors and as such believed they should be the only ones to dispense vitamins. But they sold like mad.

# The Calico Collection
## (or 'stuff' as APG would call it)

ANOTHER SEASON THAT was fun to design and a dream to produce was the Calico Collection. It solved the problem of accurate sales forecasting, as it was a fabric you could use over and over again without making an expensive commitment to buying specially made material. It was easy to match with broderie anglaise lace and ecru satin ribbon for threading and trimming.

Calico had always been used as a *toile* to test the pattern and shape of a garment before it was made up properly in the expensive fabric. And I had always loved the look. I discovered at South Down, our house in the country, that the Bloomsbury set had used calico for dustcoats and over-garments when riding and walking there in bad weather. There were beautifully cut riding coats, side-saddle skirts, jodhpurs and over-dresses just lying about in cupboards of the house. These were rightly given to the V&A before we ever lived there. But I had seen them on a couple of earlier lunch visits, and I was entranced.

Using them as inspiration, I made everything in calico – smock dresses, low-waisted frocks with gathered, flounced skirts and, best of all, provocative hotpants with matching broderie anglaise frills, bloomers and Liberty bodices, all very short, which sold faster than we could make them. With the white nail polish, palest chalky pink lipgloss and dark eyeshadow under asymmetric bobs, this was a hell of a look. It was washable by a good laundry or dry cleaner and outrageously pretty, although no girl looked old enough to buy a drink if she wore this in America.

# Aussie Imports
# and Jon Bannenberg

THERE WAS A wave of empire builders, reformers, and adrenalin junkies who came in from Australia in the sixties and seventies. Many of them were brilliantly talented and provocative – but you should never have any two of them round to your place at the same time. They were very jealous of any other new imports and wanted to protect their potent Aussie wit and keep it to themselves. They needed more elbow room than any other people I have ever met. So the Chelsea set each adopted one Aussie wisecracker. They tended, like most sensible immigrant, to start in Notting Hill Gate.

These Aussies were great performers, chefs, comedians, writers, piano players, designers and wits – mostly male, though of course we must not forget Germaine Greer and Pamela Stephenson who are still both terrific powerhouses. There were many artists among them who were part of the Pop Art movement and became very successful and influential. All these Aussies were a huge new source of energy in London.

Jon Bannenberg was our Aussie friend and he designed our third shop in London in what was the wrong end of Bond Street. He also designed for me a wonderful studio house I wanted to build in the Alps of the South of France where the food was delicious. This is where Briard dogs herd flocks of sheep in the low mountain pastures and dig out the truffles that make the perfect omelettes in the local bars. This caused my love for Briards and all my troubles with Ferdinand, of which more later.

The house Bannenberg designed for me was to be built in a remote part of France. It was to be in the shape of a snail shell, with a huge studio living room on the ground level, and above it a bedroom area with an open fireplace, duplicated below. It was to have a domed glass roof looking to the stars. In fact, most of the studio was glass, allowing one to stare down at the stunning view of Ramatuelle nestled in the foothills of the Alps. The area is full of sheep and truffles and nothing much else. It was a fabulous design. Jon had insisted that he could design the house for the same price as the old village house I had been looking at and contemplating buying.

When the quotes came in, it was to cost about fifty times the price of the village house. 'Don't worry,' said Jon. 'We will build fifty of them and sell them.' Jon's wife was furious and I was heartbroken. Jon gave me the model instead.

# Crêpe

I LOVE HEAVY black crêpe, partly because it is so chic, but also because it is so perverse when it is used in sharp, tailored shirt-dresses. I especially like it stitched with several rows of contrasting white thread, jeans-style, and accessorised with a heavily stitched black crêpe tie belt with a buckle, trench-coat style. I wore such a dress to the Savoy on the day I had to speak at the Woman of the Year celebration in 1963. So subtle was this brew of black crêpe shirt-dress, opaque tights, flat long vamp shoes and Vidal Sassoon bob, that the doorman would not let me in. 'No hat,' he said. 'You can't be speaking at this convention.' But yes, I was.

We produced this exact dress again just a couple of years ago and it sold like mad in Tokyo. I have one still.

You can use crêpe in several ways but here are the four best.

The first is a dress with a circular contrasting collar, cut on the cross, and similarly circular cuffs that drop over the hands, clown-like.

The second is a double crêpe dress, with two flounces that fall from the neck over the shoulder, and a contrasting fine rouleau (rolled) bow and tie with long ends that hang down the front of the gently shaped dress. This is called 'Daddy's girl', for obvious reasons.

The third is a simple black dress with a white Peter Pan collar sitting away from the neck, and lots of pea-sized, covered buttons and crêpe loops to clasp at the wrist. This dress is deviously appealing and was adored by Audrey Hepburn amongst others.

The fourth is the heavy black crêpe shirt-dress I mentioned above, with a collar, wide double cuffs and a wide tab front. All finished with contrasting white stitching. It has a wide crêpe tie belt to be worn tight or loose.

Any one of my four favourites would work forever.

# Dinner with Nureyev

MY FIRST MEETING with Rudolf Nureyev was not very auspicious. After the introductions had been made and we all settled down to a delicious dinner, Carl Rosen, my American manufacturer, leant across me and said to Nureyev, 'Tell me, what do you do?' After a horrified pause, Nureyev managed his famous leap from a sitting position and flew the restaurant, never to be seen again.

So I needed to have a second go.

A grand party given by the American journalist Fleur Cowles and her fourth husband Tom Montague Meyer was held to honour Nureyev and Margot Fonteyn after we had seen one of their mega performances at Covent Garden. Champagne and canapés flowed when suddenly a shriek went up from Nureyev: 'Meat, I must have meat! Red meat, no, I mean *raw red meat*!' It made me realise the immense input of energy demanded by dancers. I have never bothered to eat canapés since.

I met Nureyev again in the South of France, at an intimate private dinner party on the night of a heady heatwave. Our host owned a handsome young Irish Wolfhound, which was everyone's delight.

The doors and windows of the house were opened to allow the air in, but then suddenly everyone realised the dog had gone, no doubt straight out on to the huge main boulevard running along the seafront in Nice. We all dashed out, leapt into cars and yelled his name in despair, but to no avail. Hours later, driving along forlornly, still looking and trawling as far as Beaulieu, APG and I saw a chapel on the beach. It was lit from inside by hundreds and hundreds of candles, flickering in the most dramatic way, almost as if the whole building were on fire. The main double door was wide open. We went in.

The chapel was built in a Baroque Italian style and inside it was full of life-size wax models of the Madonna and Child and Christ on the cross. There were dozens of huge ornate candlesticks as well as the small classic Catholic candles. Nureyev had clearly spent some time there, setting up the lighting and presentation for his private performance with the dog. He had lit the lot. But on seeing Alexander and me at the door as an audience, he renewed his energy and enthusiasm, and, surrounded by these macabre wax figures and dramatic flickering candles, the pair danced as to death, until both Nureyev and the dog flung themselves to the ground, panting and gasping and laughing, rolling with wild pleasure together.

Two totally freed and crazed creatures dancing and leaping together.

# What It is to Be French

USING THE FRENCH technique of gaining an undercoat tan on a topless beach near, not at St Tropez, I would sunbathe most of the day whenever I was in France. One day I noted a terrific French girl whose breast implants did not turn over properly as she moved, so they always pointed straight up. Apart from me she gained no attention from anyone all day. In the late afternoon sun, she sat up to get dressed and first put on her espadrille wedge sandals, paying great attention while tying the ribbon bows around her ankles. She then stood, shaking back her hair and applying her lipstick. Only finally did she put on the rough black cotton lace frock over her head, shimmying it into place. It was only as she dressed on the beach that every male watched, riveted, having lain next to her and ignored her half-naked all day.

I remembered a twelve-year-old French girl asking me, as a designer, which was sexiest – a one-piece or bikini? She herself insisted that a one-piece was better, and with the most sophisticated shimmy, she demonstrated how to roll down a swimsuit on the beach when sunbathing. She was devastatingly right.

It is no surprise to me that both girls were French.

It is style that makes a woman erotic, not the clothes themselves.

# Photographers

PHOTOGRAPHERS ARE ALWAYS very strong, positive characters, which I suppose they have to be to get the results. Some use pushy abuse and some seductive charm to make their victim react. Bailey is the pushy one, insulting you into life.

Norman 'Parks' Parkinson, however, has a gentle flirtatiousness that works. Parks also had an elegant certainty about him that made you respond. Parks would offer to lend you his beautiful house in the Pacific Islands – he was an amazingly kind man with an enchanting wife and son. He always arrived with the picture he wanted ready in his head.

Cecil Beaton always directed the photographers taking pictures of him, and so every photographer would arrive at the same Cecil Beaton shot. He had worked out how he should look and be years ago, and made them all stick with it.

Terry Donovan was a genius with lighting for photography and television. He made retouching afterwards unnecessary and so kept total control of his photographs. He obviously believed in protection and drove a tank-like vehicle all over London. All the other photographers admired and respected his immense skill.

When John Adrian was doing a shoot with me, he set up a huge looking-glass in front of me, and let me get on with it. It's probably why the results are so flattering, as the pictures reflected my self-indulgence that day.

Women photographers tend to make you feel as though they are doing some research for private medical insurance. I find it very rattling and I don't like it. They can be so intrusive.

John Cowan had the best 'hello' I have ever come across. He could make you feel that to meet him, just then, was the one thing in the world you most wanted. I have known at least two other people like this and it is a very rare talent. If you are on the receiving end you find yourself offering invitations and suggestions like mad, which two hours later you don't know how to refute, and climb out of.

John's passion for fashion was laced with excitement about new architecture, so he was always encouraging models to leap out of things. His muse was Jill Kennington who was a great model and a very clever beauty, and was always prepared to leap somewhere unusual. She is now an extremely good photographer herself, which is great because she has such a depth of understanding regarding fashion.

Most of the sixties fashion photographers learnt their trade while doing army service. The army had modern photographic equipment and they were encouraged to learn and practise on it while they were training. So instead of lying on their camp beds on Salisbury Plain every night, they took up photography and it became a career afterwards.

Most of the wonderful fashion photographers I had the good fortune to work with would say they learnt from John French. In fact some had even started off as his assistant. John French photographed most of my early designs, so he had an enormous effect on my success. He set the style for fashion models and strongly affected the whole sixties fashion mode. He could also photograph a pair of shoes or a pair of knickers alone as a still life and make them memorably powerful images. Many are used to sum up sixties fashion to this day.

# Perfume

THE PERFUME WORLD is a collision of high-powered laboratories with vast production factories based in Paris, plus old-fashioned lorries loaded with flowers, arriving early in the morning in Grasse, the perfume capital of the world, which lies inland from Cannes. It is in Grasse that the early stage of development takes place, the final marketing and detailing going to Paris, where chic American *Vogue*-style women and traditional Gitanes-smoking French men sit around green baize tables, flexing their noses. It is a world steeped in tradition and very set in its ways.

The idea of developing a Mary Quant perfume was a great excitement to me. Like my cosmetics that went before, here was an opportunity to do something really new, something revolutionary. A large board meeting was called. Discussions went on. With lawyer-like precision, briefs were written for all the five or six major perfume suppliers in Europe and sent to Paris, Grasse, Zurich and Geneva. The perfume was to be very young, very fresh, very Mary Quant. After a great deal of work from competing French companies, they came to London with their samples, all of them desperately disappointing. They were sweet, boring and *pointless*, old-fashioned 'toilet water' scents, nothing like we had wanted at all. What had gone wrong? These companies were the best. They developed for Chanel and Yves St. Laurent. Everyone agreed it must be the brief or perhaps the translation.

So off I went to Paris and Grasse myself, taking a few words of my appalling French and my PA with her grossly limited schoolgirl vocabulary. Once there I soon realised that our carefully prepared brief meant nothing to these perfumiers: the fashion revolution that had swept across London and beyond had not taken root in France. The perfume business was still dominated by men, in spite of Chanel. The experts, the grand noses of the perfume world, still had a 'Daddy's Little Darling' view of what 'young' meant. Mini-skirted and determined, I had to convince them that my perfume needed to be radical – sexy, chic, the epitome of the young career women who bought my clothes and wore my make-up. It wasn't the translation that was wrong but the *idea* in these Frenchmen's minds of what young English girls were like. I had to provoke these stunned, complacent, but hugely skilled and charming middle-aged men into realising that we needed to produce something utterly original.

That wasn't the only hurdle. In approaching them, I had gone against the unwritten rule of Perfume Etiquette, which stated that any new perfume could only be produced for established French fashion houses and established French brands. You couldn't develop any new approach in perfumes for a British or American company – only derivatives of established French perfumes. It was, in effect, a closed shop. Sensible French, looking after their own interests as always. I had ruffled indignant feathers. But this was a battle I had to win. I didn't want their prejudices, but I needed those noses.

We sat round vast baize tables, the size you find in billiard halls, while they puffed on Gitanes, and together we sampled and sniffed on spills and talked scent and the perfume business. We discussed the old French classics: Chanel No 5 – now totally associated with soap, it's so copied. Diorissimo – civet musk. Bandit – great name. Cabochard – interesting. L'heure Bleue – over-rich. We looked at them from a modern perspective, trying to identify what they lacked. We also looked at men's perfumes and toilet water – why were they so popular with young women? I wanted our new scents to be open and confident, like the men's scents, but also female, sexy, daring and complex. I wanted an erotic feel coupled with a kind of cleanliness, in the sense of salt seawater on a young girl's skin.

One of the experts seemed to grasp the idea of the new, emancipated, independent and ambitious young women of our market, as distinct from the old dream. Soon, with his expertise, some totally new and provocative perfumes started to arrive – potent, animal, civet. Another of the big companies started to grasp the idea and followed suit. We were in business.

We arrived at three distinct perfumes and chose three names, each capturing the image we were trying to reflect. Two of them summed up the day-to-day lifestyle of the young working women who bought Mary Quant: A.M. and P.M. The third perfume, which came a little later, epitomised their attitude, the thing they were causing in the streets and in the bars, at home and in the workplace: Havoc. This scent was open, sexy and potent. Havoc was not only a great name in itself (suggested by businessman Torquil Norman) but a hell of a seller. It was a huge success, particularly in the Middle East and Dubai. I started to wonder whether they were drinking it. We didn't launch in Japan to begin with, because in those days the traditional Japanese idea of perfume was that it was only used by people who did not bathe. The Japanese only used perfume in secret, although you could stand around at Charles de Gaulle airport behind a queue of young Japanese tourists buying bagfuls of the stuff.

After the launch and success of Mary Quant A.M. and P.M. and Havoc, there was a rush of new, overtly provocative, sensual perfumes launched internationally, which was fun to observe. We had broken the mould again.

# La Colombe d'Or

TWO WONDERFUL THINGS happened at this time. I had invented a new type of perfume. But I had also discovered La Colombe d'Or.

One of the best treats of the fashion business is that you have to go to the most delicious cities in the world and then you have to go again – twice – the following year. So welcome to the delights of Como, Milan, Venice, Paris, Barcelona, Madrid, Nice, New York, Hong Kong, San Francisco and Tokyo. Of all these heavenly places, Saint-Paul de Vence probably takes the biscuit.

It was the French perfume industry that first introduced me to the Colombe d'Or hotel and restaurant, and I fell in love with it right away. The first thing that greeted me was a sign, in French, which read 'When you have arrived at the Colombe d'Or – you have arrived.' It was put there by François Truffaut. But nobody told me that.

Madame Roux, the owner, orchestrated everything from the log fires to the oil lamps outside. Every morning, dressed in black, she surveyed the scene from the top of the village of Saint-Paul de

Vence, to judge the weather in order to decide whether lunch was to be laid outside on the terrace or inside the dining rooms, where there are the most sensational paintings from the likes of Picasso, Braque, Miró and all. Legend has it they were left to pay the hotel bills run up by the artists, who also gave painting lessons to her husband.

The summers that I was working with the perfume developers and buying swimsuit fabrics, I used to take my design work with me to Provence and set up base at the Colombe d'Or. It became our second home. The cast was irresistible. Simone Signoret lived there at times, working on her memoirs. On a good evening she ran the bar, elbows on the counter in front of the Matisse murals. She was designed for the role. Yves Montand played boules in the square outside and flirted with the village girls. Picasso's ex-wife, Joan Miró, Graham Greene, James Baldwin, François Truffaut and Catherine Deneuve were all regulars, and later Sting. Lunchtime could be equally good, with Joe Losey and Marc Chagall in attendance plus David Niven for wit and wisdom. Madame Roux liked me because I swam in the pool whatever the weather, and she hated to see the steam rising from an unused pool on the frosty winter days, knowing how many francs were burning. I have the same feeling nowadays with my pool and can become quite edgy with guests if they won't go in.

My working day was perfect. I would have an early swim followed by breakfast, then work or draw for my next collection until 2 p.m., when it was time for a long indulgent lunch amongst the favoured, along the sunny wall of the hotel. Nice airport being so near, we even held Mary Quant board meetings at the hotel, between two stained glasses of Marc's situated at either end of the pool. I would chug up and down, doing my lengths, while all was discussed. I remember one Christmas morning walking barefoot through deep, deep snow to swim in the pool, which was surrounded by fruit trees, still bright with ripe oranges.

Even years later, when our son Orlando Plunket Greene was a baby, we stayed there regularly. He would sit in his chair up on the windowsill by the main door, orchestrating events with a celery stick while he sampled the day's menu. In the late afternoon, Alexander and I could wallow in the fine art collection at the Galerie Maeght up the road and be back for drinks at 7 p.m., with OPG sitting on Madame Roux's lap at the entrance, welcoming all her guests. We also had our nanny Bryony with us, who was the perfect Mary Poppins. This must have given Orlando the training for later in life, when he accompanied us on our visits to chateaux all over France, photographed by Brian Duffy, for our wine business, with him sitting through long lunches in a baby chair aged two or three, with six wine glasses in front of him while he ate coq au vin. The difficulty arose when this became his view of work: grown-ups spitting out wine or sniffing perfume spills, testing make-up or trying on sample clothes and not going anywhere.

I remember one last batch of samples worked on in Grasse had to be delivered to the airport in Nice and flown back with us to London. They didn't arrive in time and we had to check in and go through on to the tarmac without them. Suddenly a voice shouted from above on the viewers' open terrace and with wild enthusiasm the sample supplier burst through the crowd and threw the packages to us down below, having just managed to catch up with us.

Alexander and I caught them and were immediately set upon by several Niçoise police, who appeared out of nowhere and herded us back into the airport in front of the large audience. The flight was held while the police tested the samples to make sure they were legal. But on seeing their Provence-Grasse label, they immediately escorted us on to the flight and insisted on upgrading us to business class. Lesson: always have your samples made in France.

After the launch of the three female perfumes, a male scent came next. The best nose in the French perfume industry was obviously the man to develop it. This very flirtatious Frenchman caused consternation within the company, but he also developed new products that ricocheted around the whole industry, causing outrage, scandal and delight and pushing the world of modern perfume into previously unchartered territory.

We didn't stop there. Soon we were developing 'Make-Up for Men' – foundations, moisturisers and tanning products – a whole range. This caused extraordinary shock at the time, although it was so obviously needed. It was a colossal success in all the Scandinavian countries and achieved a staggering amount of publicity everywhere. Stanley Picker's cosmetic company, Gala Cosmetics, who made these products for us, was thriving and out-growing its space on the Surbiton bypass. I still remember the pride I felt seeing the Mary Quant daisy flag flying there as I passed by, early every Monday morning.

Then came the horror and madness of the Three-Day Week, which destroyed everything. How stopping work could save the economy is an idea too extraordinary to contemplate – but not to Mr Heath. There was no shop lighting, factories could only stay open three days a week, even television companies were required to stop broadcasting early to conserve energy. Utter madness reigned. London (and my hopes) plunged into darkness.

Happily, the Colombe d'Or remains a perfect corner of heaven and is immune from change and the vagaries of fortune. It is stuffed with blissful memories for me. Somewhere in its deepest cellars there is a suitcase full of my design roughs and drawings, which I left by mistake. The hotel is now a favourite of Ringo Starr who has scrambled eggs for lunch with Parmesan on top. I like that too.

One more story from the Colombe d'Or years. Tax was ruinous in Britain at this time, and after paying over ninety per cent tax on your earnings, you could only take £25 out of the country. There was also something called a dollar premium, which you had to buy into, and pay a further forty per cent tax if you wanted to be allowed to take any capital out. I wanted to buy or build a house in France so, enraged by this, I took a wodge of my hard-taxed earnings in my knickers to France, and put this for safe keeping into the security box at the Beaulieu Hotel reception desk, where we were staying at the time.

On the next trip over, I asked the hotel manager's assistant, who was on duty, if I could have my package. 'What package?' he said, looking me much too firmly in the eye. It was then I discovered what arm wrestling was like, as I stared back at him, sat down, crossed my legs and said: 'My package, please.' Well, I won, and leapt straight in a cab after paying the bill, not returning the bundle to risk having to fight for it again.

So there I was on the way back to Nice Airport, returning with the currency once more. I had an important meeting with Mary

Quant Cosmetics next day, and it was the night of the moon landings. I'd planned to watch this on a television set outdoors back home in England, so that we could also be looking at the moon at the same time, celebrating with champagne. What could I do with the money? The Colombe d'Or, I thought! It was mid-summer, blazing sunshine, the hotel swimming pool would be full of guests. There must be someone there I knew that I could leave it with. Arriving at the hotel's pool, the Alexander Calder mobile looming over the steps, I spotted an artist friend, but no Madame Roux.

'Hello, keep that for me please!' I yelled, and threw him the package and drove on to the airport. Two years later the money was needed to pay for the house and I went back to ask him for it.

'Oh God,' he said, 'I'm afraid I've spent it. Things have been a bit tough.'

But, poor chap, he paid it all back faithfully bit by bit and I felt rather cruel about it. This was the money I planned to build a studio house with, way up in the mountains back from the coast at Gréolières, where the truffles come from.

# Special Recipes

THE MINI-SKIRT MUST be more popular in Italy than anywhere – as the cheers I used to get from customs officers when crossing the border into Italy were similar to a soccer-style standing ovation. So the launch of Mary Quant Special Recipes was a huge occasion to be celebrated at a very beautiful vineyard in Tuscany.

Special Recipes was an idea I had for a second Mary Quant make-up brand, made with largely natural ingredients of flowers, herbs, fruit and vegetables. It was conceived at the height of 'flower power' in the late sixties/early seventies. The whole concept was nostalgic and the packaging was old-fashioned and romantic. I wanted black and gold chunky pots and jars, with sympathetic rounded graphics, in black, mustard and gold. It was very successful, but the manufacturers did not want to pay us a further royalty, so after a couple of years it was only sold in Asian countries where it sells extremely well to this day – although of course the ideas were assimilated everywhere.

The launch ceremony for the press was in the afternoon. Our host was the owner of the vineyard in a vast wine-growing area. He asked me would I join him in the morning to judge the best village garden competition. This was highly prized every year. So I went with him, going from house to house, making notes and accessing the loveliest gardens.

Italian village gardens are completely unlike our English cottage gardens. This is the land of terracotta pots arranged down the steps and along the terraces, each more stunning than the last. At every house we were invited in to sample the owner's home-made wine and delicious bruschetta and tutti-frutti tarts. These were placed in front of the two of us, sitting alone, while the *signora* stood on the other side of the table studying our reaction. The rest of the family, the father and all the little children, would stand arrayed outside the door in rapt, concentrated attention, watching our faces on tasting.

The home-made wines were not at all like the ones produced in the commercial vineyards. Their own wine was highly fortified and of dynamic strength. At each house this ritual was repeated with intense concentration. I realised this was deadly serious. There was no French-style tasting bucket. I looked to the vineyard owner with growing anxiety as more and more houses and gardens and wines were 'studied' and sampled.

Finally we were left alone to compare notes and contemplate the winner. It was only then that the elegant vineyard owner of this vast chunk of Tuscany admitted that the winner had to be the head manager of the whole estate and that he won the competition every year. Reeling with wine and delight we drove away with everybody happy.

In the afternoon launch for the press, the Special Recipes

make-up arrived loaded on top of a hay wagon, drawn by two handsome oxen. It was led by huntsmen in full hunting gear, and trumpeted by hunting horns and hounds. The whole Italian presentation was fabulous and added to my love affair with Italy.

# Tug-of-war at South Down

BY THE LATE sixties, APG had finally bought South Down, the house he adored. It had been built in 1928 by his favourite great aunt, Flora, who he so admired. Final negotiations were entered into with relations who had inherited it for a while and then moved on and bought their own favoured houses.

A housewarming party was demanded. The local police team had just won the national police tug-of-war competition. This seemed a good extra excuse for a celebration. A marquee tent was ordered, the garages turned over to ice-cream parlours, the house was opened up and the garden devoted to children's entertainers and other delights. An Irish barrel-top painted caravan, my birthday present, was devoted to gipsy fortune-tellers. The front door exhibited all the silver cups and medals that the British police tug-of-war champions were proud to have won.

APG persuaded George Melly, a jazz band and a rock group to perform in turn all afternoon. Conjurers and magicians wandered around. Hot dog stands, pizza stalls and goodies were arranged here and there in the garden, with beer, wine and champagne available everywhere.

We had invited the triumphant police team and their wives and friends and most of London's top international fashion models and photographers, along with most of the fashion people we worked with and all our old friends. A tug-of-war was to take place at 4 p.m. between the police team and the mini-skirted models, their boyfriends and all the male models they knew.

The September day was perfect. The conjurers and magicians were wonderful, the pizzas terrific. The jazz band with George Melly competed in turn with the rock group, and won on rude jokes.

As promised, the tug-of-war took place as billed with the top models, who had a more robust team of male models and fashion photographers, fashion artists and journalists in their team than one might have expected. The models – I won't name them, as they are far too well known internationally – lined up on one end of the rope, and the champion police team revved up on the other end. The cows mooned over the hedge to watch the sport.

After a couple of false starts, the jazz band revved up for a final effort, two farmers and four heavyweight cricketers joined the model girls' team, and the battle commenced. The police champions won – but gracefully, not too well. And an interesting selection of mini-skirted models, policemen champions, male models, boyfriends and policemen's wives disappeared off into the hedges and fields, sharing their favourite pills and ciggies as they went.

Buster the dog rounded up everyone before dark and a convoy of police cars, with sirens blaring, guided everyone home and back to London. The tug-of-war silver cups were safely removed and the September harvest moon rose high in the sky.

And so the house was christened.

IN 1970, THE giant British manufacturing company ICI made an extraordinary proposition that I should design a coordinated home furnishing set, consisting of a duvet cover, a wallpaper design and a stretch cover for armchairs and sofas, plus paint colours that would also harmonise with the designs and work together. It would mean working with four different subdivisions of the company and bringing them all together. Duvets were almost unknown in this country and France, and were really only used in Scandinavian countries and Germany. ICI wanted to make them popular here.

Alexander and I had already lugged an enormous duvet back from Norway by plane, having loved the pleasure of sleeping under them in Scandinavia. We were already converted. In those days you could only buy plain duvet covers, hidden away in a single deep drawer at one store, Heal's, in London.

At first I turned down the proposition, saying that fashion design was my role and I didn't know the furnishing market. But ICI insisted. 'We want to bring fashion into the furnishing market,' they said, 'which is why we have asked you.' It did occur to me then that, yes, I did want to buy the same fashion colours and patterns that I used on my clothes for our apartment, and that, yes, I would love to specify the Dulux paint colours to go with it (Dulux was owned by ICI). And what's more, I wanted an Old English Sheepdog to go with it too.

Coordination was the new watchword in design. Having designed so many fashion pieces that were meant to work together – for sportswear, work or play – the idea was natural to me. It was like visualising tunic dresses, skinny rib sweaters and pantyhose all worn together. It was simply coordinated sportswear for the house.

The timing of the ICI deal was perfect, as the washing machine was becoming the new booming household essential, and duvets made bedmaking easy. The new career girl was our customer, so this was a lovely design job for me. The gingham wallpaper became a classic for many years. It had a frieze of gingham on the cross to coordinate with it.

The first package was so successful that the various manufacturers working under the ICI umbrella wanted to go on with many more designs, whether it was paint colours, soft furnishings, wallpaper or whatever. The problem was that each manufacturer wanted equally noisy designs because it would gain them photographic exposure for publicity, but of course it was impossible to coordinate four equally gasp-making ideas. Which was to be the cool brand? Some of the manufacturers would arrive in their own private aeroplanes. I remember complaining I was becoming a psychiatrist to their needs: balancing the macho egos of these mega-manufacturers became quite a problem. Alexander came back from lunch one day followed by a Le Corbusier chaise longue for me to lay my clients on.

Indeed we did buy an Old English Sheepdog pup. We called him Buster. Alexander collected him from Terry Donovan's studio in Knightsbridge where he had been photographing the dog's famous father for ICI's Dulux paint. The breeder used to bring father and pup to London for photographic sessions, by train, first class, from the north of England.

Buster would commute with us at weekends from our house in Alexander Square, Knightsbridge, down to the country. Driving back every Monday morning, the suburban houses on the Kingston bypass looked exactly like vintage thirties wireless sets. They have developed charm over the years. (In the same way the Ford Ka today looks very like a fashionable trainer boot, while a mobile phone looks to me like a cosmetic compact.)

We'd let Buster out on the way home for a run in Richmond Park, until he had rounded up the entire flock of sheep that was kept there in those days. Later we lodged a flock of sheep in the country to keep him happy, and so his commuting days were over. He took well to country life. He grew bigger and shaggier and loved jumping gates, hedges and especially horse jumps. He was a born show-off and hogged every photo opportunity.

I used to ride in Richmond Park too, and one day I was invited to ride with JC Penney's head man in London. Foolishly accepting this offer, I discovered he kept a horse there and was an extremely proficient rider. He was of Native American Indian extraction himself and I am sure his horse was as well. I did not go again; I couldn't keep up.

Thanks to ICI, I suppose I was one of the first designers to see that all trends – colour, texture, pattern, shape – start with clothes fashion. We buy what we love, and like to repeat the pleasure again and again when buying other things, whether they are household objects, gadgets or soft furnishings. Fashion anticipates the mood and it has the advantage of having shorter lead times than cars or mobiles. Fashion is always out there ahead, testing the waters. It can be the victim of its own success and quickly be thought boring, or it can become classic and be reinterpreted with small variations over and over again – like the mini.

# Design

STUDENTS ESPECIALLY ASK me: 'What made you design clothes?' This question always stumps me because it feels as though the question should be: 'What would it have taken to *stop* you designing clothes?' I could not stop. There was a stage when the more I did, the easier it was to have ideas and the better the ideas were. This is probably a sign that one is at the peak of one's ability. I was putting down ideas at a nonstop rate for clothes, shoes, socks, undies, knitwear, coats, hats, bags, stockings, shoes, carpets and make-up. The more ideas I put out, the more they came. And the finished result looked exactly like the original idea. The manufacturers, the cutters, the people I worked with, so understood my thinking that the results became more and more accurate to the concept in my head. The thrill was enormous; to have an idea and be able to transmit it, to have it sampled, polished and then produced by mass-production methods, and to see this rolling off the machines, shown in shop windows in other countries, photographed, worn and enjoyed, is ecstatic stuff. There is nothing else quite like it.

However, this is where problems often start. Seeing this seeming

My favourite dress –
"Banana Split".
Grace Coddington
was a favourite model.
This dress worked
day or evening.
The image became a
Royal Mail stamp.

Bazaar, our first shop. I loved doing those windows in the beginning, usually at midnight on Saturdays. People would flock to see the new windows. London couturiers egged me on.

Twiggy: how she could dance!

Coddington takes to "The Footer"

Pattie Boyd picks a Stone.

Parky picks a tie.

In Milan, "The Peter Pan" collar became "The Quant" collar.

---

MQ cosmetics — black, white and silver packaging. Colour was the product.

In the Ball Room
studio in London,
sporting the
MQ collar.

Portrait of me in
Harris Tweed,
by the great
Terry Donovan for
Wool Board adver

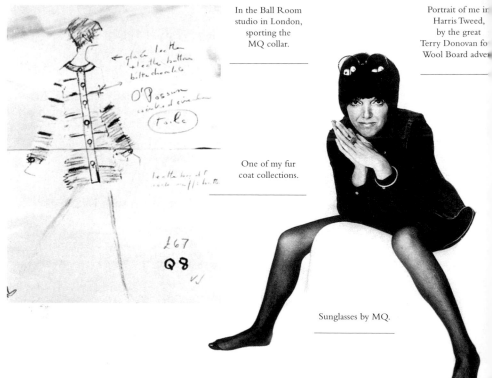

One of my fur
coat collections.

Sunglasses by MQ.

# Where does Mary Quant get her style?

## Wool.
## It's only natural.

Certification Trade Mark
PURE NEW
wool

The Wet Collection:
PVC designed and
made in the
Chelsea studio.

ease, the management side of a fashion business invariably comes to feel that anticipating the next fashionable shapes, textures and colours should be logical and not left to the designers. They start drawing up graphs and lead times, working out what the 'next thing' should be. They then insist on briefing you, the designer and the design team, on what the 'next thing' is and how you should do it. It is a form of jealousy: after all, to see one's ideas becoming reality and mass-produced is orgasmic. If it was not happening to me I would be damned jealous too, so I completely understand this feeling and how it starts. And of course there are some logical ground rules, like knowing your clientele loves high necks or low necks and long sleeves, and one learns to develop these points into a collection. But fundamentally where fashion goes next is like studying the weather – there are so many moving and changing variables. You cannot predict it on a graph.

Did that colour, that texture or that shape sell too well and become hackneyed, pointless and boring? Or is it something that will always work and flatter, in which case you need to think of a new way to do it, so that it looks brand new. 'The same but different,' was the dreaded phrase always put to me. 'I just want the same but different,' they would say, not realising that this is the most difficult thing to bring off. Of course you want that as well. But the guile and the gift lies in how you do it. What do they think one is thinking about all the time? The same but different, and revolutionary too – OK!

So I would go into a trance. Drugs would probably help, but no – a glass of red wine is more reliable. I always had a vacuum-cleaner mind. I only see what I want to see. A colour or colour combination or texture, that I wasn't seduced by a few weeks ago, suddenly becomes overwhelmingly attractive. Certain proportions, certain ways of tying and wrapping and closing things, will start to haunt my mind. A mix of tough and soft or languid. Too big or too small – shrunk – both can look very young. Big, big buttons can make you look thin but tiny buttons can also make you look sweet or fastidiously elegant. Country shapes in fine evening fabrics work well and keep everyone on their toes.

The same but different:

A Norfolk jacket in crêpe jersey is different.

Jodhpurs in satin or crushed velvet is different.

Dungarees in moire taffeta or silk jersey.

A suspender belt in tweed with rubber suspenders.

Jodhpurs in georgette.

French bloomers in mohair.

Frilly flounced clown collars and cuffs in Prince of Wales suitings.

Peter Pan collars in plastic.

Cricket pads in black satin.

I did them all.

The joy of making things out of your head and seeing them everywhere is like hearing 'Yesterday' pouring out of a jukebox in somewhere exotic like Peking or Verona. Bloody marvellous.

# 'Real Men'

REAL MEN DID not like babies. They leaked at both ends, were very expensive and distracted women from their proper role of looking after their menfolk. Men were bent on making money and having fun. Babies changed the power base altogether and took attention away from them. Babies were tiresome and much better avoided.

However, avoiding pregnancy was difficult. In fact, avoiding pregnancy tended to dominate relationships before the Pill. Real men tended to be rather bad-tempered about pregnancy. The usual solution was to produce the money for an abortion and send the girl to a couple of doctors' addresses in Chelsea and Kensington, while the man would take a break in the South of France. If she insisted on having the baby, he would usually put the girl out to grass until the whole thing was over and then reconsider his options.

Like his father before him, Alexander Plunket Greene had always said he did not want any children. I took this to be a masculine aberration, which would eventually be grown out of. When I became pregnant and had a dramatic miscarriage, this was fine for him but felt like appalling misery and failure for me. That feeling went on for what should have been the entire length of the pregnancy and settled down into simple despair afterwards. But I became pregnant again in 1970 and quietly got on with it this time. I told very few people and went on working even harder since I felt absolutely terrific. I thrived during a promotional trip to Sardinia and Venice. But on a further promotional trip to Ireland with JC Penney for a photo call, I had to crank up the starting handle on a beautiful old Hispano-Suiza motor car. The car failed to start and I failed to feel pregnant anymore. I was in pain and convinced I had miscarried again. I mourned this terribly and took to my bed. Everyone else went off to the Curragh Races in County Kildare, leaving me behind in disgrace, as no one knew why I was ducking out of the outing.

Some two or three months later I rather shamefacedly admitted that I did still feel pregnant after all. My GP and gynaecologist rushed round to our Chelsea flat and joyfully announced that I was four or five months' pregnant. With my yellow ochre Moroccan trousers and black patent leather Japanese clogs drawing everyone's eye, no one had noticed I was getting bigger and I felt jubilant. But most of the businesspeople we worked with were furious and the manufacturers we worked for were outraged. Even business journalists who had enjoyed having a woman to interview and photograph for the City pages (because a woman was rare on those pages then) were outraged. It is a strange feeling to be attacked by someone you don't know. I suppose if you know them you start to rationalise their dislike straight away, but with a stranger you feel helpless. One manufacturer wrote to me expressing his shock as though I had misbehaved. I was in disgrace with all our licencees except one – Alexon, which was owned by the wonderful Steinbergs, a proper rag-trade Jewish family who sent ecstatic messages and flowers and champagne, and hugged me with tears of pleasure pouring down their faces. Alexander Plunket Greene and Mary Quant had made it.

I bought a paperback book on pregnancy but only read the months I had already survived. We had moved to a house in Alexander Square by this time and painted everything white again, except the top floor, which I painted a very subtle terracotta, so as not to provoke the vibes. I longed for a boy. I bought no baby things at all, trying not to challenge fate. A few days before the impending birth a great friend, shocked, went to Harrods and bought everything vital on my account. Harrods to the rescue again.

I went to work every day and was much enjoying my broody mode. The weekend before Orlando Plunket Greene was born, we went to a village Guy Fawkes party, during which the pub caught fire and burnt down. There was a stampede. Two days later I knew the baby was on its way. I went to work as usual but left early and bought two white towelling dressing gowns and a meat pie, which I pushed into the oven, hovering over APG while he ate it. Then I burst out for the first time: 'It's all happening – drive me to the hospital!'

We grabbed a bottle of champagne and drove to St Teresa's, a Catholic maternity hospital. Opening the bottle and making jokes about my pubic hair shape, we downed the champagne and APG left, not to be seen again for two or three days. Orlando was born too early but beautiful. He was put into intensive care while the journalist Jean Rook, who was tailing me at the time, sat downstairs praying for drama. Three days later, just as the afternoon sun went down, Alexander arrived in my room, pulled back the sheets and got into my hospital bed with me. Without saying a word, he went soundly to sleep. And so did I.

A few hours later, in the black dark, the door opened and there stood a priest. Above his head hung a bare electric lightbulb, illuminating his hallowed head. I shut my eyes and waited. He stood there for a long time praying, then crossed himself and very gently shut the door. I always wondered whether he went down to reception to report a man in my bed or to book me in for next year.

# New Fabrics

JUST AS WE are breeding new dogs such as Labradoodles and so on, we are also constantly developing more and more new fabrics. I managed to achieve some of these fabric mixes after great battles – my bonded jersey and crêpes for instance. My knowledge of making hats and ironing veils into the bevelled shapes I wanted meant I had no fear of the stretch fabrics that were being developed at the time, which terrified many manufacturers and designers. Dry cleaners would say, 'I don't want to dry-clean Mary Quant clothes because she uses funny fabrics.' But my hat-making experience – with its artificial flower-making, varnishes and curved surgical sewing needles – made using this fabric second nature to me.

The idea of creating fresh mixes has really got going now, which is thrilling; so now we can have fabrics with the lightness of georgette, the toughness of linen and the delicacy of silk. These fabrics also have the ability to take colour, clear and pure. They can also be made shower-proof at the same time, or drip-dry. New fabrics are now being developed with bubbly seersucker effects, in silky satin finishes and with a touch of stretch. The textured lines I wanted to have with crease-resistance are a cinch to make these days. Silky mother-of-pearl surfaces can give subtle glamour to the soft surfaces of fabrics that have never been seen before. We can even produce crazy combinations such as PVC mixed with a wool-like fabric. There is no end to the design fun possible with these new fabrics and mixes.

Fabric manufacturers have also at last seen the advantages of adding slogans to the selvedge (the self-finished edge of fabric), incorporating phrases like 'I love you' and 'Plain sailing' or adding a provocatively pink edge.

Silky, textured aertex drapes seem perfect for summer. These new fabrics enable one to design chic, draped garments that are sporty and tough and glamorous. I love the mix of sporty, chic and sexy at the same time: wonderful. So greedy and delicious.

# Nanny

FINDING THE RIGHT nanny is one of life's more disturbing experiences, so I can't believe our good fortune in finding Bryony.

Bryony had a beautiful smiling face, naturally pearly pink nails and the deepest gurgling laugh that could not be matched. She moved with a slow confidence that I did my best to emulate, and played guitar – one tune only. She loved French and Italian food. And best of all, her father was a Master of Wine.

Bryony and Orlando adored each other and so did I. Alexander and I were travelling the world launching my cosmetics, fashion and bed linen. I would not travel anywhere without them all. No one else but Bryony could sit through five-course lunches in French châteaux, with six separate wine glasses, silver and china, and hold their own with colossal charm, all the while keeping Orlando sitting like Churchill at the table. Everybody loved Bryony. She had been trained well by her father.

Her father suggested we start a wine business together, which was a pretty irresistible idea. He worked with one of the biggest and most important wine shippers. Together they saw there was a new market opening up, selling good, everyday drinking wine to women and delivering it to their homes. As in the motor-car industry, male salesmen would not bother to take seriously any women who wanted to buy and order wine, unless their husbands started the account. Banks were the same; they would simply not discuss money or mortgages with women.

Attractive as this wine idea was, it worried me because it was very different from the clothes, the cosmetics and the duvet covers I designed. We were buying from established vineyards with their own labels and merely introducing the wines. It had not been done before. However, the business was very successful, stimulating the wine stores to understand this new female market. Television, getting wind of this lifestyle, wanted to come with us too and make a documentary about it.

Madame Bollinger was one of our best suppliers. She understood immediately the new female market. Champagne was not selling as well as it does today and it was this new market that so boosted champagne sales later. Madame Bollinger rode a sit-up-and-beg bicycle with a basket front and back, with lots of strings to protect her skirts from the wheels. She wore pearls and a double-breasted suit and riding skirt in what looked very like a good Scots tweed. Madame Bollinger went early every morning to see the vineyards and arrived back in time for champagne and lunch. She was one of the most contented and witty women I have ever met, who enjoyed her family, her friends and her wine. She seemed to have cheated death by anticipating rightly the pleasure her wines would deliver years later. It seemed to me that wine was a hugely attractive business, a mix of cooking, designing, farming, marketing and fashion, which is why it is the easiest way to lose money. Every element has to be right, including the weather.

Madame Bollinger's château had a soothing, tempered quality that reminded me of Colette's house, which Chanel had lived in later. I felt the three women had a lot in common, including their shared love of champagne.

# The Little Black Dress

THE LITTLE BLACK dress that goes anywhere and everywhere is the most appreciated garment in a woman's wardrobe, and the most fun to design. Because it has such precise limitations, it is an interesting problem to design one's way out of.

It reminds me of art lessons at junior school where on the last session each term, the art mistress would say, 'You can all paint anything you like today.' Nobody could decide what to paint and argued and messed about, and we slowly realised we all felt disappointed. Limitations are madly provocative and should be enjoyed.

A little black dress that I particularly loved designing was superficially very severe and surreal. The dress was made of black crêpe, long-sleeved, with slit pockets either side at hip level, as on trousers. But one side had a very elegant hand-shape appliquéd on in gold kid. The hand was padded to give it a rounded, bevelled effect.

The neck was severely boat-shaped with a drill of five gold bead-shaped boot buttons on one side on the shoulder. It could also be worn with black crêpe narrow trousers, Capri-length, with gold boot buttons either side, at the hem. It still works today.

The most successful LBD I ever designed was called Banana Split. It was made of black jersey, always a good start for any time of day. The body shape was gently curved, flaring from mid-hip level, then flying out into a three-quarter circle skirt. It danced, this dress. You only had to stand still and sway. It had a white stand-up collar with points to the ears, and a zip running down the centre to pubic-bone level. It was tough, sporty and dressy – all at the same time, in black and white. It was the one used on a British stamp. This dress would still work today too.

On one model, Grace Coddington, who's now Fashion Editor at American *Vogue*, I drew the daisy on her navel as a pièce de resistance, so when the zip was pulled down, there it was. The daisy would appear. We have a photo of the dress, but unfortunately it's not unzipped.

Grace was always my favourite model. She even managed to keep that Wellington-boot walk of hers that sealed the triumph of her performance in the American *Vogue* film, *The September Issue*, in 2009. It's her mixture of fashion know-how, beauty, stylish simplicity and total sexy self-confidence that's so attractive. Japanese girls tend to have something of it too.

# Travels with a Baby

WHEREVER WE WENT, Orlando came too. I learnt from him how best to travel: if nothing is happening just go to sleep. And if you are stuck in an airport just spread your books, paper and crayons on the floor and get on with your drawings.

I learnt to have design meetings with my artwork or samples spread out on the floor in airports and railway stations. I remember spreading squares of carpet patterns on the main floor of Charing Cross station and in hotel reception areas.

I have spent many years believing in the importance of freedom for both partners in a marriage to have their own careers. Both also need to be able to cook, to drive their own car, and to have their own bathroom. Both need to be able to look after the child and both need their own room to work in alone, as Virginia Woolf said a hundred years ago. Both need to pay for things roughly equally and neither should make their partner work impossible hours. Both parents should make huge efforts to be fun for their children – though some women become jealous of the children's affection for their partner, as often the man can be more riotous and amusing in their play. This sort of boisterous play is good for both sexes – it helps girls become more outgoing and generous and boys become more thoughtful and less demanding because they learn that there is someone bigger and better than them. But equally children must have the space to find amusement themselves, on their own. This seems to be a major problem today, as people fear children can never be alone – but alone is very important. And children don't get a chance to experience it.

I was lucky as there cannot be many nannies as good as Bryony or my later superwoman, Jenny. As Nancy Mitford always said, children who don't have nannies are very boring as well as bored and some training is needed for a nanny to be very good at it. Following Japanese principles would be a start. The Japanese adore children but don't indulge them. Their children have to live in this grown-up world, not the other way round.

# Hats and Hair

HATS ARE WEAPONS: divinely flattering, imposing and triumphant. Hats suggest special times and for weddings they are the personal piece of cake. One of my many great memories of Orlando and Bona's wedding was the blissful arrival of Jasper Conran, driving his open-top Bentley with six delicious models and beauties, including his stepmother, all wearing hats – chic hats, wild hats, Parisian hats. They are the ultimate statement of pleasure. The fact that they are unnecessary makes them even better.

How important are clothes, style and image? Clothes get there first. It's the clothes, the walk, the hat, the hair, the gesture that I look forward to seeing when first meeting people. From then on you are qualifying that. But it's the first effect that is so compelling. Even when you know someone well, it's what they are wearing that tells you whether they are in a good mood, or whether they are feeling anxious or depressed.

The first effect can well be subtle and underplayed but it should always demand interest. It's a pleasure to dress well: one of life's little treats. The subtly clad, chic woman suggests voyeurish good taste.

She makes one want to find out more about her. The extrovert dresser, on the other hand, looks for wit and fun and attention. Clothes and fashion have a powerful ability to make one what one wants to be, rather than the nervous, introverted character that surfaces at four in the morning on a bad night when you can't sleep. Get the clothes right and one feels happy, confident, extrovert and generous-minded. Get them wrong and one feels miserable and mean-spirited. Some clothes never let one down and however old they are, you know you always enjoy your day when you wear them. But something new makes you feel sharper and more aware and gives such zest to life.

Elsa Schiaparelli designed the best hats. I know how romantic those big, floppy, ripe, summery hats can be, but a Schiaparelli hat is dynamite. She knew if you tip a slightly soft doughnut of a hat over one eye, you have got it. Irresistible.

Kate Middleton is someone who knows how to wear hats at the right Schiaparelli angle. She is immensely attractive, slim and stylish and looks as though she enjoys it all. This lets Prince William off the hook, which must be a great relief for him.

One of the pleasures of hat-making was chasing around London to locate the tiny firms that made ribbons and trims and decorations for hats. It was called matching, although that was the last thing you did: you were looking for provocative bits. Dashing past the wrong end of Bond Street one day, I saw this photograph of a haircut that stunned me. I had never seen hair styled like that before. The sign on the window said 'Vidal Sassoon' and apparently he was miles upstairs, reached by a rickety lift, capable of carrying only one person or, more suitably, food. But up there he ruled, cutting hair and performing, rather like a four-star chef. I braved the lift, sat there and simply watched. I did not have the money for a Vidal Sassoon haircut that day, though I knew I would save up. This determination was hardened by a woman who turned out to be an actress called Jill Bennett who, seeing my long, thick ponytail, shouted: 'Don't do it!'

But I did.

Vidal Sassoon completely changed hair. Before Vidal it was simply hairdressing. Vidal made it cut and style. He saw that, like architecture, hair could be cut into shapes and textures that not only flattered the character and texture of the hair, but projected the best qualities of the head and face − pointing out the cheekbones and focusing on the eyes and making the maximum impact on the individuality of the face and personality. In the Japanese erotic tradition, he also focused on the back of the neck. As one of the great photographers said to me after a session: 'Of course, Vidal Sassoon invented the way you look.'

Vidal not only created the most famous and important of his cuts, the 'five-point', which so clearly highlights the eyes, cheekbones, nose, mouth and neck, but he went on to develop more and more revolutionary variations and developments. Asymmetric or en brosse, I had them and enjoyed them all, as so many of us did. With extraordinary generosity he set up Vidal Sassoon schools and taught everyone about his haircutting techniques and style. There is no country in the world that you cannot find a Vidal Sassoon disciple to cut your hair. He left this legion of stylists with a legacy of confidence to go on with their own ideas, developing and experimenting with the fun of the new.

Vidal Sassoon liberated women from the punishment of hours spent under the bonnet of a hairdryer, with fat rollers skewered to their scalps, while being par-boiled. We found the freedom to swim in the sea, drive in an open-top car, walk in the rain and then just slick our head under a tap and shake it to look good again. Your hair did not forget the shape and chunky curves he created, and it simply returned to base.

Vidal Sassoon, the Pill and the mini-skirt changed everything. For me, Vidal Sassoon produced the perfect cap on my leggy mini-skirted designs and the frame for my Colour Cosmetics.

Any taxi driver in London will tell you he grew up with Vidal Sassoon or he had him in his cab. He will then go on to tell you that Vidal is the nicest man in the world. And then he will say, 'By the way, your barnet looks good!'

Vidal Sassoon is a bit of a performer and when he gets going he is a hell of an act. It was said Vidal liked cutting my hair because I have a double crown and that gives the right bump on the back of the head. He was cutting my hair in the Bond Street salon late one evening to promote his five-point cut. There were press photographers there and all of Vidal's top stylists, plus Alexander because we were going out to dinner with *Vogue* afterwards, with Clare Rendlesham no less. So Vidal, spurred on by the vast audience and the presence of Terence Donovan, and with several press cameras flashing, went *whap* and cut my ear. Not the whole thing but the fat bit, the lobe, and nothing bleeds more than that. Vidal made like it hadn't happened, dabbed harder and talked faster while waving his scissors in ever-larger circles – but nothing would staunch it. Blood spurted. APG, watching, said: 'Vidal, I know you are

Jewish but vengeance for the lampshades is not necessary.' The whole place collapsed laughing.

When Vidal Sassoon was opening his first salon in New York, which must have been one of the most terrifying and important days of his life, I was also showing my collection in New York that day. He offered to cut my hair at six o'clock that morning so he would have time to do it for me, and did. That's friendship.

# Design Things
# That Work for Designers

GARDENS SHOULD ALWAYS be designed to make you look around that corner and make you ask, 'What happens there?' I like vistas to be crossed with interesting gates, hedges, walks and trees – again to make one go forward and look further. It works in a similar way that a complicated sponge cake, with sugar on top and chocolate in the middle, whets the appetite.

The same thing applies with design in fashion. A superficially simple look that demands analysing is the best, so that the observer's attention, after the initial glance, is held by small surprises and extra detail. The head-to-toe look must balance, but the style of the jacket, the skirt, the pants and boots, etc. are like the hedges and gates across a beautiful view, and the accessories are the points of interest that finish the complete look.

Most people have an ideal skirt length that flatters their own leg, which is why the old question of how many inches above the knee you should go is just irrelevant. Besides, why stick to one length that is deemed to be 'in fashion'? Ultra-mini, loose-fitting dresses look great with cycle-length shorts underneath. There is a knickerbocker length just over the knee that is ideal and a Capri crop-pants length, worn with ankle boots, which make a feature of the gap of leg showing between them. Or how about the chunky calf-length boot, which has a rather adolescent zap, classic-length riding boots, or over-the-knee boots or socks? All these cut-off points on the leg can be balanced with your skirt and pants, but you should look for the ones that both flatter and surprise. I love leggings worn with open-toed ankle boots. The slight suggestion of French prudery is fun.

Skirts with ruffles that just shadow the knee from above are flattering. Can you see or can't you? Inverted box pleats can suggest a matronly look but on a very short skirt they have the opposite effect when they are placed at mid-thigh. Very short bloomers can be fun, as can flattering French knickers or a high bikini cut. Capri-length pants can be emphasised with striped socks or black opaque tights worn underneath, and high wedged espadrilles or boots with ribbon ties round the ankle.

Hipster belts and jewellery worn high and low on the hip, or corset-like belts around the waist make another defining focus and marching rows of buttons or zips can point the eye where you want it to fall. I love to use sprat's head stitches in a similar way, to get attention. The same design fun can be had with puffed sleeves, double cuffs and floppy ruffles. You can train the eye where to go. It is good to have the narrow belt back these days. One can get the waist effect without the rib-killing problem.

The most delicious collars are never pressed flat but instead curl up gently from the base of the neck. The Peter Pan collar is the most flattering ever devised. I was very pleased to discover it described as the Mary Quant collar in Milan by the fashion trade.

I have often used a variation of hunting-style stock tie-necks and DJ and evening-dress bow ties in my collections, as all are very flattering. It would be crazy for men to abandon these; they all have such classy sex appeal. The open neck is only attractive when it is used with a deliberate look of abandonment, but becomes boring and unflattering if it is used too regularly. All these necklines also flatter women, giving a dashing, emancipated look. But women reserve the right to revert to the appeal of cleavage, when in the mood. Very flattering for women is the high white piqué (lightly textured) collar curving up to the ears, but starting with a very low 'V' front.

The square neck also has huge appeal when you are young but it can look very severe later. The boat-shaped neckline is surprisingly flattering. The wrap skirt with a curved hem at the wrap is always a winner, as long as you can make it young-looking by keeping it short and accessorising it well, or making the top black and the skirt white.

A note to would-be designers: always put a little too much design into your first samples so that you can give some way under pressure.

# Japan

ON OUR FIRST trip to Japan in 1972, Alexander, Archie and I were thrust into a press launch. The fashion journalists were all male and wearing identical black mohair suits. They carried black briefcases with zip tops, out of which came cameras. Like a chorus line they went snap, snap, snap. First question – always one spokesman only: 'How much money do you make and what is your turnover?'

Answer? 'We don't know.'

Amazement.

End of interview and end of press conference.

The second trip to Japan, arranged in London, we were given an intense schedule covering two weeks, with meetings every half hour, day and night, for the three of us. On arrival we were driven straight from the airport into a conference in the head office of our manufacturers, where we were given a completely new schedule in which Alexander and Archie were not included. They were told, 'You are welcome to do whatever you like. Tour Japan – Tokyo, Osaka, wherever you want. But we only want Miss Quant. It is so extraordinary to have a woman in her position.'

The interviews were arranged for every twenty minutes of every day. Apart from an interpreter from the Japanese embassy, I was alone. The petrified female interpreter, who had only limited English, was soon overwhelmed by the situation. Luckily a very bright Japanese student, doing holiday work for the company, stood up and said in fluent English: 'The interpreters do not understand – let me.' She soon became my right-hand woman.

The impact Japan had on me cannot be understated. The dress, colour, attitude: all overwhelmed me. In the 1970s, Japanese women still wore kimonos in the streets and certainly at all formal functions. Nothing is more erotic than traditional Japanese geisha dress. It not only shows great beauty in itself and appreciation of the female form, but it gives off a subtle suggestion that its wearer is out of bounds, belonging to someone else and too expensive for you.

And of course there is only one key: pull the sash and all will unravel.

There are several levels of geisha. With the maiko apprentice geisha, traditional clothes will exaggerate her youthfulness and helplessness; the clogs are so high she cannot run away; the kimono is lovely but understated; her face will have very little make-up. The sash of her kimono is untied and flies behind her as she runs, harassed and late, to work with her colleagues, giggling and covering her revealing mouth.

The graduate geisha has fabulously expensive and beautiful layers of kimono, so heavy and valuable that they have to be lifted by a professional dresser. The sash is tied. And although it only needs a single pull for all her many kimonos to unravel, this can only be done by her owner, who has bought her years ago and paid for and directed her many years of training. She is the ultimate symbol of male desire, testosterone, ownership and financial success.

Most daring to me is the geisha cosmetic tradition. The face is porcelain white with a small ruby-red mouth and well-defined eyes. By contrast, the naked back of the neck exposes the bare, natural colour of the skin. This erotic flash of the neck, framed by the brightly coloured dipped collar of the kimono defies all European ideas of make-up, and so shocks with pleasure.

Dining out is very important to the Japanese and I have rarely experienced such second-hand pleasure as when being graciously dined and fêted by my business partner, Nakayama-san. Not knowing quite how to amuse a female guest, the Madame restaurant owner geisha appeared on one side of me and the novice geisha trainee appeared on the other in their desire to please me. I was a heroine to all of the geishas, because of the prestige it meant for them as women in having an honoured guest of their own sex. The usual geisha's job is not only to please, amuse, flatter and look after the guests but also to fill the American and European men's glasses so regularly that they tend to get drunk. Meanwhile they water their Japanese patrons' drinks. The geishas paid me the same honour and watered my wine. And the food was delicious.

Parties and receptions were easy to handle despite not knowing the language because the bowing and introductions on both sides took so long that you could fill a whole evening without saying anything at all. Grand dinner parties were rather more difficult because of the Japanese passion to tease their guests. Fish eyes, fish jaws and slugs can throw one a little, because if you don't eat it, they can't eat it either, and they want to. They like fish eyes. It's their food. So you lift the exquisite lid of your delicately delivered bowl with some trepidation.

On my first visit to the restaurant where Churchill once ate, I had Orlando, still just a baby, with me. He sat within my crossed legs on the floor in the proper, formal way. After lifting the lid of each bowl before me and discovering more fish eyes or slugs, I lifted whatever it was with my chopsticks and deftly put it into Orlando Plunket Greene's open mouth like a little bird. Down it went. After a few such dishes I looked across at his father's distraught face. He had no such willing dustbin. I suspect Orlando's love of Japanese food probably dates from this subterfuge. The food is the best in the world and the Japanese appreciation of it is entirely justified.

Over time I was treated to meals at the greatest restaurants in the country. The restaurants devoted to the blowfish season are the most expensive and unique. Every tiny course of this banquet is devoted to the blowfish. Failure to remove the poison sac from the fish would be lethal so one false move from the chef and you would die. Even the wine has a blowfish fin dunked in your glass. The raw marinated fish makes smoked salmon seem crude. Its excellence is established by whether you can see the pattern of the plate through the finely sliced fish. Further courses consist of different pieces of the blowfish cooked in varying ways. On one visit, the climax of this delicious meal came with what seemed to be small rolled cheese balls that tasted exquisite. My London PA, who had come with me, congratulated our hosts on the perfection of this delicacy, but foolishly asked what part of the fish this cheese was made of. 'The testicles' came the answer. She fled, shoeless, from the place.

Small children are adored and worshipped in Japan, as they are in Italy. We had with us our most brilliant nanny Bryony, whose father was a Master of Wine, as I have mentioned, so she was equipped for all purposes. On the second day of our first trip to Japan, the telephone rang and a voice said: 'Do you remember me? I am Simone, the scrubber from your King's Road days.' She was an old friend of ours who I had known years before. She went on: 'I'm now married to our man the ambassador in Tokyo, so I am used to young children. I will send the embassy car every morning while you are here and pick up Orlando Plunket Greene and his nanny and they can have a lovely time here in the park and pool of the British Embassy garden. Otherwise they will be bored stiff.' So every morning this huge embassy car arrived with the flag up front and off they swept to the British Embassy. My days were spent bowing and meeting store managers, drinking endless cups of tea, discussing with manufacturers the idiosyncracies of American, European and Japanese sizing, being videoed and interviewed constantly, or visiting stores. I did wonder quite how I had ended up with the wrong job while Orlando Plunket Greene had the right one.

Small Japanese children have a strange, doll-like way of sitting, immobile, with their feet straight out in front of them. Businessmen take their children with them to work by train. Years later, I was on the commuter train in the rush hour from Tokyo, towering over the businessmen as they bowed knee-deep to each other, holding it for so long they nearly missed the train. I spotted a little child sitting innocently next to his businessman father, calmly reading a comic. I looked at the comic from the other side and saw it to be the most extreme pornography, drawn in such graphic detail, I could not believe it possible. I bought a copy of it in the railway station on my way back. It was so unbelievably rude, I sent it care of Bryanston for Orlando and his dorm-mates.

When we came to my station, there was my colleague to meet me, the carriage being perfectly lined up with the numbers on the platform. Why can't we do that in Europe? We were chauffeured to the workplace of the craftsman who was printing and placing the artwork from our London studio onto the lampshades being produced here. I was shocked by the cell he worked in, with only a grid in the ceiling for light. His studio was the size of a broom cupboard. I accepted some coffee, which turned out to be the pre-war Camp coffee that comes in a bottle like Worcester sauce, with boiled milk! Ah. We checked the placing and the colour of his work was correct and I was embarrassingly picked up by a huge limousine and taken off to a very expensive lunch.

Soon it became important to go to Japan three or four times a year, taking the designs and discussing the samples that would be produced on the next trip. During my early 1970s visits, some British manufacturers I worked with came too and we all went to Kyoto together, to visit the Japanese company that printed and manufactured my designs for sheets and bed linen. This was a hugely modern factory but with a traditional family background. The entourage of men accompanying me became larger and larger, and the competitive tension culminated in a duel between the two MDs, as to who could perform more and more complex calculations the quickest – the British man using his pocket calculator, his Japanese counterpart his abacus.

Needless to say, the abacus won.

By then I was staying at the Okura Hotel – my Japanese partners were very generous as this was, and still is, a wonderful hotel, especially if you are using it as a base to work from. I learnt to enjoy staying Japanese-style there and developed a tremendous love of Japanese ways – their food, saunas, swimming pools and beds. Japanese beds, rolled out on the floor, are the most comfortable ever. And the big dome-like bauble of a computer mouse on the floor beside one, controlling everything, feels very powerful. I love the importance given to the ceiling design, and the lapsang souchong smell of tatami mats makes the floor a pleasure. The Japanese only ever look down, except when they're in bed looking up, so they understand the design significance of floors and ceilings.

I love also the Japanese idea of only having objects that you need, which work efficiently and are beautiful in themselves. I am always surrounded by clutter. Clutter is the way I like to start work because pristine expensive paper is too inhibiting. But out of the clutter of swatches and colour comes the final design, honed down to a single idea or ideal. I then only see the design, and become surrounded by clutter again, which I don't see.

I once spent two weeks working from the Okura and doing interviews there. I rarely went out at all, except sometimes at night I would walk the back streets for exercise, from my Japanese-style Okura building to the Western-style Okura building some blocks away – up and down dead escalators and past shuttered shops, seeing the reality of Japan. In Japan you are incredibly safe, which is very liberating for a young woman on her own. There were little factories in this district making the imitation food to put in restaurant and café windows for you to choose your menu, and tiny tempura restaurant bars that only had seats for about six people. They would cook your order for you individually – mostly vegetables dipped in batter and quickly deep-fried. Delicious.

Later, British Airways asked me to write a piece about my favourite hotel and I raved on about the blissful merits of the Okura, saying it was the best hotel in the world to work from. After my review on my next visit I found the manager and his entire staff had lined up at the front door to welcome me, bowing in unison and whispering, 'Very nice, very nice.' From then on, every evening, two beautiful young men were sent to my suite of rooms to make up my futon bed in the direction I liked, and to run my bath, open a bottle of champagne for me and switch on the television. I realised then that I needed a Japanese wife, or preferably two, and even better if they could be male.

At the weekend my treat was to go to Mount Fuji and stay in a traditional hotel overlooking the mountain. This was thrilling but at six o'clock in the evening the telephone went and a voice asked how many beds I wanted to be made up in my room. 'No, please,' I said. 'I'm here alone, so just me.'

But the voice said, 'What about your colleagues – all six of them, and male?'

'No, no, no. Just me – one bed, please.'

Cue despairing voice on the other end. What everyone else did, I had the sense not to enquire.

I had been told to ask to see the sunrise over Mount Fuji, so I ordered breakfast at dawn. Breakfast arrived, perfectly timed, to be eaten on knees. Fishy rice and one orange, semi-peeled, so that one only had to pull the last coil. Table and cushions were arranged for the perfect view. All in place with two minutes to go before sunrise – fabulous.

With the early morning swims, saunas and Japanese food, I have never felt so thin and in such good nick as when I was in Japan. This was just as well, as the work schedule was prodigious, with design meetings all morning and the afternoons taken up with promotional interview after promotional interview, all at those rigid, twenty-minute intervals. My brilliantly clever and fluent Japanese student interpreter became so good at the interviews that she came to know all my answers. 'Give them number forty-six,' I would say, and she would reel it off. Some evenings we dined alone and I could ask her all the many questions one longed to ask about Japanese life, Japanese marriage, Japanese sex, Japanese men and Japanese politics.

Most Japanese journalists were male, and as the interviews progressed I began to notice the questions were gradually becoming more political and more sexy, and more and more journalists were turning up. It dawned on me that my interpreter had achieved a sort of transference, where I was off-loading the stress of so many interviews on her and she was enjoying a ready-made platform to voice her own views, an unusual treat for a Japanese girl. Thanks to her, my answers became increasingly politically informed and increasingly provocative. We had developed a sort of brilliant double-act. It must have been surprising for them that I seemed to know so much about Japanese politics and opinion.

The design team developing our ideas in Tokyo all looked like schoolgirls and we would go out to lunch together in a crocodile formation. I would occasionally catch sight of myself with them in shop windows and think, 'Who is that funny-looking foreigner?' It didn't end there. We sometimes danced the night away in the chicest discotheques, taking the Mary Quant Cosmetic staff with us. We just threw our handbags in a heap with everyone else's, forgot about them and danced. In the background there would be videos of baby animals playing – puppies and kittens dressed in fashionable baby clothes and expensive jewellery. The bars sold delicious, fresh, chilled food, and the music was a collage of jazz and rock.

I was amused and delighted by the way these young Japanese girl assistants would give me delicious, expensive knickers as birthday presents instead of the cakes or flowers we would have in this country, all divinely packaged and decorated with a real flower on top. Of course the Japanese are marvellous at packaging – the shop assistants there will wrap your purchase for you with such care, attention and finesse that one feels incredibly clever to have bought oneself a present. It's very effective.

On one trip to Japan I went to one of the main university areas to see what the students were wearing. There I came across the most seductive little sweet shop. The shop was tiny but all the windows were crammed with glass bottles full of loose sweets. Humbugs and barley sugars, bull's eyes and liquorice all-sorts, acid drops and sherbert in clear bottles with thick glass stoppers. There it occurred to me that the perfect and most attractive way to stock and show cosmetics was as if they were sweets. This thinking led to the Mary Quant Colour Shops, of which there are now over 200 in Japan.

With three or four trips a year to Japan, I developed a passion for the sushi bar in Shibuya next to the Mary Quant head office. The bar had a male chorus-line of chefs chopping in unison and exploding with a 'Hi!' at the end of each order. The most extrovert chef had grown up in England and seemed to have trained in the Boy Scouts.

Once, fortified by such a lunch, I just made the flight to London, when we were suddenly found to be on a detour to Copenhagen with forty minutes to waste there. Trapped in the departure lounge, I became aware of a potent emotional atmosphere. We seemed to be surrounded by small Danish families, all waiting in a frisson of anxiety and silence. There was the certainty of something traumatic about to happen. A flight landed outside the windows and the last twelve arrivals to disembark were all nuns dressed in black, each carrying a small swathed bundle and an even smaller brown paper bag, with no luggage. Peering surreptitiously, I could see that each bundle contained a very small newborn baby with black standing-up hair and a label stuck on the blanket. Each bundle was ceremoniously handed over with a bow to one of the small, fraught families. Nothing was said. The nuns returned to the plane and we were called for London. I had never experienced such intense electricity and such silence in one forty-minute delay. I still wonder how those babies thrived. It seemed quite fitting that Denmark is Hans Christian Anderson country.

# 'Beautiful Chrysanthe'

JON BANNENBERG HAD everything, including his wonderful Australian wife Beau Bannenberg. Jon offered to lend us his flat in Athens for a holiday after our tough trip to Japan, and not only that but he also offered us the services of his Greek PA, who came in every morning and could achieve tickets and invitations to anything we wanted in Athens – she was a Greek toff and beautiful.

Life with Chrysanthe's help was terrific, a breeze. When she was going off for the weekend to her uncle's house on Hydra, she told us he had left the key in the village shop for her. 'Come too,' she said, 'you ought to see some of the islands.' She went ahead and we arrived later by boat on Saturday evening. There she was, standing on the harbour to greet us, with a photographer who took some happy snaps.

Chrysanthe's uncle's house was heaven. It must have been the harbourmaster's house as it dominated the view of the harbour, so one could watch all the large boats come in. The house was five or six storeys high, each being built in a completely different century of Greek architectural style and decorated and furnished to complement each era. It had no plumbing but instead it had a well and a shower and lemon and fig trees in a secret garden on the ground floor, as well as a wine cellar and kitchen, dining rooms and bedrooms on the different levels. We had a delicious weekend with Chrysanthe and several boyfriends of hers. We swam in the sea and ate in the most delicious fish restaurants on the rocks. Seeing how much we were enjoying Hydra she suggested we stay on alone till next weekend and then come back to Athens. Great idea – we bought lots of wine and food and settled in.

By Friday we had fallen into a delicious pattern of sluggish bliss. We would swim all morning in the transparent sea and enjoy a late lunch in the perfect fish restaurant. The restaurant boss would arrive for his own late lunch at about four o'clock, by which time the waiters had collected up all the fish eyes left on their customers' plates into the huge bowl for him to devour in bliss. This became our signal to retreat back to the harbourmaster's house for a sexy late-afternoon slumber.

Climbing back up to the door that Friday we opened it to discover a strange, tense atmosphere. Outside the top master bedroom a very small, excited man appeared, shouting in Greek and clutching his pyjama pants, which had lost their vital string and kept failing him. A very strong female voice behind was delivering his script. Several languages were tried and what it came to in each was: 'What the hell were we doing there in his house with our six large suitcases covered in Japanese labels and filled with sales samples of much of the Mary Quant winter collection for Japan?'

Alexander Plunket Greene apologised and offered Gauloises and glasses of wine – but the Greek had no hand for it and became even more excited. Chrysanthe, his niece, was mentioned, to no avail. The harbour photographs were produced but he had never seen her before. He had no niece.

With appalling embarrassment, apologies and offers of money, we retreated in as dignified a manner as possible, dragging our suitcases out of his bedroom and down the hill to the harbour, barely in time to catch the last boat out to Athens at five o'clock. Neither of us said much on the boat back but as our taxi delivered us to the Bannenberg door we did feel sheepish.

Out of every door and window came the blazing sound of music and a vast orgy. We dumped our bags and fled out to dinner. Chrysanthe had clearly wanted us out of town – we were limiting her style.

We didn't speak to Chrysanthe again until some months later when she wrote asking for the agency for the Mary Quant collection in Greece.

# Japanese Models and Japanese Girls

JAPANESE GIRLS HAVE just the sort of looks that I most enjoy designing for. They took to my designs and my make-up ideas straight away and understood them. It must have hit Vidal Sassoon in just the same way.

Japanese girls tend to look much younger than they are and for much longer. They have a very good body shape, fabulous ivory-coloured skin, perfect high cheekbones, dark eyes and glossy thick straight black hair – a treat for Vidal Sassoons cuts. They are athletic and move well and avoid the overtly Hollywood, self-conscious sexiness that television and film promotes here.

Japanese children learn to draw, paint and write from the earliest years of infant school. They are allowed razor blades to sharpen their pencils and crayons and are taught how to paint – how to fill the brush with colour and press lightly and then heavily. I wish we taught children like that in this country. It is much more attractive and satisfying than telling them to 'just press the button'. So they study and appreciate handwriting, drawing and painting, all of which gives so much pleasure. This is why the Japanese often appear to study your name and address card for so long.

Young Japanese men enjoy and understand fashion in the same way, and appreciate good quality clothes.

Japanese women are very intelligent and well educated, yet while they are young, they are always described as the assistant to a man and treated as 'the flowers of the office', even when they are the ones actually doing the job. As soon as they marry, which is as late as possible, they become almost unemployable. They usually move in with the husband's parents and are bullied for the rest of their days by their mother-in-law. It seems it is only in television studios that young women are allowed to be in charge. I was very grateful that my Japanese business partner Juichi Nakayama had two daughters and no sons, so they were allowed authority.

The good looks of the young Japanese girls are based on their cheekbones, and I could see what inspired Vidal Sassoon's greatest haircuts. The country was made for him. I had a similar advantage with my designs, as, once they were given the confidence, Japanese girls would wrap and wear my clothes with such panache.

Their beauty is stunning.

# Testosterone

IN MY CHELSEA studio we developed a huge design package of house and bed fabric designs, which our Japanese company adored. This we tuned and developed for America as well, after an introduction to the market by the fashion consultant Nigel French. Huge quantities of samples and books were produced and looked delicious – when testosterone struck. Nigel French fell out with his male business partner and they just threw everything at each other. At the same time – this was the early seventies – my Japanese partner Nakayama-san decided the fabric design package was somehow 'riding on the back of the Mary Quant cosmetics'.

I have never been able to understand this thinking – I don't love a fabric design because I use the lipstick, but that's how it felt to males. This was all before Tom Ford, who would think it laughable logic. Nevertheless, the home team insisted I pull out, so as not to upset Japan. The luxury soft furnishings company Dorma, who owned the rights to my designs under the ICI deal, had a lot more sense, and promptly sold them to Marks and Spencer without my name. They also sold them in the domestic and French markets under the Dorma name. The best sellers would suddenly be removed from sale and reappear in M&S.

Well, I have always admired M&S, as I have JC Penney, so what the hell, but I would have liked to have achieved at least half the royalty. Tom Ford has probably done a lot to clear the thinking, but as I was first in with the design brief I was given by ICI ('Put fashion into fabrics – duvets, bed linen, furniture fabric, wallpaper and paint colours please'), I was rather ahead of my time. I had first thought I didn't know enough about these products, but quickly realised that design is design. I do not want last year's colour and style for furnishing fabrics and products.

Design is design and fashion its future.

# Women Today

WOMEN'S LIB HAS won. Women are in charge. Women are wearing even higher heels and wedges these days. They have broken the glass ceiling and in some cases they have broken their heads through the glass ceiling. Women are in charge – apart from in politics, although Hillary Clinton is one exception. Michelle Obama looks taller and stronger than ever if the mood takes her.

But women are not happy. Men are looking after the children a lot of the time and often they are better at it than the women and more fun too – just ask the children. The problem seems to be that women often don't like it and it can make them spiteful. Girls used to be spiteful for a short period on the brink of puberty, but now it seems to have stuck. And the most troubling part is that women don't seem to like their 'liberation' either. All that crusading that Shirley Conran and others did and women don't like the results.

Women are more polished and glorious these days than ever before. Pearly skins, glorious hair, perfect nails, toned bodies and professional-looking make-up. Women these days are expected to have the ability to handle a job, the children, the mortgage, the interior decorating, the food and the shopping, as well as looking immaculate. They have achieved everything career-wise, as well as raising children and maintaining yummy-mummy status. But they seem to prefer to spend time competing with each other rather than enjoying their partner or playing with the children.

What's wrong? They are perfect but unhappy. We can't seem to keep up with our own advances.

What happened to flirting? And sex? In Japan, men know how to really please their partner, rather than just satisfying themselves. Their oriental bathing, lovemaking and massaging skills need to be learnt in Europe and the West. It's the attention to detail that Japan does so well in all aspects of their lives. Maybe here in the West we should lay off the texting and concentrate on pleasing each other instead.

I remember driving to London and back from the country every day, sometimes in fog so dense I would have to have the car window open in order to see where I was. I would be dying of cold. Other days I was so hot I thought I would collapse in Wandsworth with still half the journey to go. Then I would arrive back in the country to find the remains of the riotously delicious day that everyone else had spent there, in the pool, drinking our wine and eating everything in the house. I would drag in the weekend food from the little Italian shop in Walton Street, before succumbing to a short kip from sheer exhaustion, wondering how I had ended up with such a rotten position, while the nannies and other mothers in my house had polished off most of the white wine and left their glasses down at the pool. I was too weary even to swim.

So how do we define the two roles of mother and career woman better? Boarding school is the supreme answer and a supply of well-trained nannies before this, but of course this is financially out of reach for most people, especially given the appalling way that people are taxed for childcare. We need more realistic taxation to encourage children to be brought up well and educated properly for the next generation. Even the French with their wonderful Napoleonic education system have trouble now. Let's get our schools at least up to the French standard and make it realistically possible for both parents to work. Then they can both enjoy their children.

Interestingly, Napoleon's wife Josephine took a royalty on the sale of all army uniforms. She was probably involved in the design of them as well. We are good at uniforms. If we took a royalty on school uniforms it would probably help pay for better schools.

These days, many men have effectively turned into the nanny if it makes more sense for the woman to carry on working. As a result 'him indoors' is becoming the housekeeper. This may turn the women into overworked, harassed monsters, but it does bring benefits: once he needed to do the washing, we had good washing machines and spin dryers. Once he had to clean up the baby, we had nappy wipes. Once he started cooking, we got minute steaks, frozen chips, tinned lentils and two-minute rice. And best of all, ready-made raspberry crumble suddenly appeared.

# Schiaparelli

IT WAS A great treat for me to be invited by the French ambassador's wife to the French embassy in London for lunch. Ernestine Carter (from the *Sunday Times*) was making a speech, and the American ambassador's wife was there too, making it a glamorously female lunch party. While I was nervously sampling some champagne, Ernestine was thrown by the horror of losing her speech and I by having my bottom pinched, very hard. I could not believe the situation, as a footman in full rig was standing right behind me. So ignoring the possibility, I turned back and the pinch happened again, but harder this time. I yelped.

More people were arriving and I heard the magic name Schiaparelli. I was frozen and, turning to a very chic woman near me, I said: 'Surely I didn't hear the name Schiaparelli – isn't she dead?'

'I am Schiaparelli,' the deep voice said. Struck dumb with horror and still feeling the effects of the painful pinch, I was further embarrassed to be placed next to her at lunch. I apologised and told her what an admirer of hers I was, having spent four hours in the deep-freeze dungeons of Harvey Nicks the week before, looking at some staggeringly beautiful coats and dresses and hats of hers, in storage for a very rich and slim women, who I think was called Russell. Although this woman had died, she had paid the storage fees for another thirty years. There were ankle-length coats made of velours and velvets, with brooches and shoulder epaulettes of fur, and devastating hats to wear poised over the nose. These were clothes of such superb arrogance and beauty. The staff had to come in and warn me I would be deep frozen myself if I did not come out soon. Schiaparelli was charmingly forgiving in her dry, gravelly way. Sometime later her niece modelled for me in New York.

Elsa Schiaparelli and Coco Chanel were deadly rivals and it is thought that Schiaparelli designed the first trouser suit, although others believe that Chanel did. But it was so inevitable that they probably both did it around the same season – when it was right.

It has always fascinated me that Chanel bought Colette's romantic house in the country as I feel they had so much childhood background in common (they were born only ten years apart and both worked in the cabarets and music halls of Paris before finding success in their chosen fields). Chanel had a very difficult time in Paris during the war and the German occupation. She tried to keep her business going, even when it meant selling clothes to the Germans. It was also believed she had a German lover. Colette's third husband was Jewish and life was very dangerous for them. Colette hid her husband in the attic of their apartment in the centre of Paris during the war, secretly travelling back and forth with him to their country house, later bought by Chanel. Colette's fame saved her husband.

Schiaparelli, by contrast, went to America during the war, leaving her staff to run the company, which they did quite successfully. She returned afterwards, doubling their salaries. It was very difficult for both Schiaparelli and Chanel to re-establish their positions in Paris after the war had ended. Both designers were looking to America. But in the USA, coordinates and sportswear dominated and America had developed a universally efficient code of sizing that would make off-the-peg clothes fit.

I'd thought about this when working in the dungeon for £4 a week making my couture model hats by hand, crafting and inventing the rounded and spiky shapes, taking two or three days to make just one hat. I'd known even then that this could not be the future.

I have always liked the immediacy and lightness of designing clothes to be manufactured in the mass-market. I understood too the importance of well-graded sizing. That was a shock to couturiers, since so much of their design work was building clothes on an individual customer's body, with many fittings and adjustments until it looked right. Designing for a commercial brand, to be manufactured in only three or four sizes, requires beguiling your customers into becoming and maintaining the body size the design needs to look good. This meant that fashionable clothes could be lighter, less structured, more fluid and sexy in new ways, which suited contemporary innovations like central heating, air conditioning and the career women's way of life. Couturiers did not want to do this as it meant working with manufacturers. This is probably why the high-fashion world was testy about me at the beginning, though they were forced to come round to the way I was working. That's what I recognised right from the start. As Helene Lazareff from *Elle* magazine and Ernestine Carter from *The Sunday Times* said to me: 'You have changed everything.'

In the sixties and seventies, everyone in Europe was thin. We were all amazed by how fat Americans tended to be. But into the eighties the same thing started to happen here, as ready-cooked food with its appetite-stimulating additives began to dominate our eating habits. So the gym and diet culture became a part of life, because the revealing nature of fashion demanded it. And career women insist on being fashionable and slim and chic.

Today couture has learnt to use the skills of mass production and enjoy the lightness of ready-to-wear clothes, without the labour and weeks of fittings or major alterations. Today women will make sure they are the size needed to wear the clothes that attract them most, from the designers they most admire. Everything has, indeed, changed.

Incidentally, Schiaparelli had a ring I have envied ever since. It was a sugar-cube size and shape in gold, and the finger went through the middle of it. It was worn on her left hand.

A Doll in riding
boots.

Lipstick colours were
never like this before.

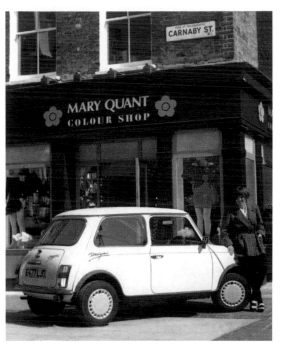

The Mini car in
Carnaby Street:
I styled its black-and-
white striped seats.

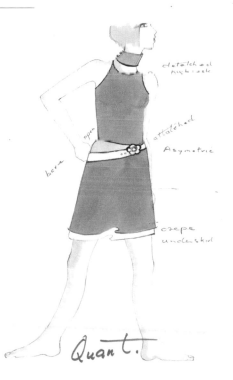

detatched
high neck

attatched
Asymetric

open

bare

crepe
underskirt

Design goes on all
the time. Dresses
sampled and made in
my studio are sent
to Japan

Quant.

Magic marker pens
sometimes influenced
the lip and nail
colours for
MQ cosmetics.

# Design and Lateral Thinking

THERE WERE YEARS when the demand for my designs in other product areas poured in because of the publicity APG achieved and the success of my Mary Quant fashion collections, and the OBE and all the press and TV attention. It was overwhelming. I took on three final-degree fabric-design students, whom I rated and whose work I had seen when I sat on the Design Bursary Awards at the Design Council meetings. This helped but the workload was still prodigious.

By then I had learnt how to rework my ideas from one area to another, so it was relatively easy for me to teach them to do this too. This annoyed some manufacturers who had taken on the very same designers themselves three months before and had failed to make it work, which was doubly frustrating for them. But they had not learnt how to skillfully resource ideas from product to product, which I had been doing successfully for some years by then. The manufacturers and their directors and accountants were also enraged by my working methods, which eschewed the use of sales graphs and charts in favour of more organic, instinctive thinking. This resulted in some monumental rows between Manchester, Birmingham and Chelsea. Some of my colleagues in the Mary Quant Company also blamed me for the rows because they did not understand how I designed.

The speed and development of the company over a few years was amazing but the stress and jealousy it aroused was awful. But I had driven myself like this for some years by the seventies and my energy was something that I had enjoyed enormously. I have always said adrenalin is the best drug in the world. It was not easy for me but it was certainly thrilling, which I suppose was maddening to others. I wanted to work day and night as well as commuting incessantly to New York, Japan and Europe. I was hooked on deadlines, which are vital to create the necessary panic. Work was more fun than fun for me.

The large manufacturing companies we worked with could see me − an individual and a woman to boot − being paid all these royalties for this huge basis of work, while they employed dozens of designers and got relatively little in the way of rights income when they were selling outside London, Paris and Tokyo. No wonder they were jealous!

# Dolls

I HAVE ALWAYS found dolls irresistible — antique dolls, wax dolls, china dolls, rag dolls and plastic modern dolls. There is something vaguely sinister about them. I used to try and make dolls as a child, using flour-and-water dough and painting it when dry. I started with finding little pieces of fruit and bread as props for my dolls' house and moved on to making the dolls themselves to populate it.

So it seemed absolutely right when British businessman Torquil Norman asked me to design a doll and accompanying clothes for his toy manufacturing company. The name took seconds to decide. 'Daisy', our trademark, was a natural.

The market was then dominated by Sindy, a British-owned but very American-influenced doll. We thought a London-look doll would be an excellent rival. Market research said yes. Nine inches was the right height. It takes a lot of agility for young children to manipulate this size doll, but there was Sindy and Action Man to prove the point.

Now, Torquil Norman is 6'7" and flies Tiger Moths and any

other aeroplane if he can loop-the-loop in it. Torquil produces lots of large children, buys large buildings like the Roundhouse in Chalk Farm and devises very small toys – Polly Pocket for one. To watch this giant run through our collection, dressing and undressing our Daisy doll, was one of the small treats of the job.

I wanted Daisy to be deliciously pretty, with an English-rose face and long, blonde, loosely curly hair. Of course her clothes would be the latest in Mary Quant-styled London fashion. I went to the famous British mannequin designer Adel Rootstein to sculpt the head and face for me, and the clothes we made in our studio in Chelsea. Daisy's clothes featured the fabrics we were using at the time in our main collection plus very lightweight denim for some rather Brigitte Bardot-style pieces. In the Hong Kong Mandarin Hotel, I sat cross-legged on the floor with some elderly Chinese gentleman manufacturers, discussing the make-up effects for this tiny doll's head, drinking green tea and explaining what an English rose complexion meant. With lots of grave bowing and nodding we arrived at the perfect look. The Daisy collection of clothes, fabrics, samples and patterns were taken out to China and copied in exquisite detail. The British manager in charge of seeing through the whole project and the production of Daisy was superb.

The Daisy doll was launched in Britain in 1973 with a high-fashion collection of clothes in front of all the most important toy buyers and the press. We showed the whole collection, life-size, on some of the best models of the day, all of whom were wearing blonde wigs and looking the dead spit of Daisy herself. The delicious Daisy doll even had a horse called Archie developed for her.

Another launch was in Finland for both the cosmetics and the

Daisy doll. It was so successful that Alexander worked out that every child in Finland had four of our dolls. We realised this was crazy and that the dolls must be going into Russia via Finland. Press people arrived at our hotel room early in the morning while Alexander was out buying newspapers. So Orlando Plunket Greene, five years old, had to let them in. 'Mum is in the boiler room again,' he said. This was my first experience of sauna baths and I was rather over-keen, so I had to rush out and explain.

We had lunch during that trip with Armi Ratia, founder of Marimekko, a designer I much admired. She had a unique way of laying out lunch, which looked so beautiful and delicious. I have sometimes used it myself since. She put beautiful bowls of raw vegetables next to bowls containing lethally sharp chopping knives for everyone to deal with their own vegetables and herbs, alongside huge basins of garlic mayonnaise. We made great friends and planned to go to Russia together to eat caviar to celebrate the Daisy doll's success. Unfortunately she became ill and the plan never came to fruition.

Daisy was a wow, and the sales were great. So much so that someone, probably Torquil, had the great idea of creating a rival. So shortly afterwards an alter-ego doll was conceived. She was different, her fashion mood black – black leather and black boots – with a Harley Davidson motorbike, studded jeans, a helmet and goggles. Starting with the same doll's head, we gave her red en brosse hair, dark eyeshadow, and a dark lip and nail colour. We tried out names in the 'Hullabaloo' direction and Torquil came up with a brilliant name – 'Havoc' – for her.

We launched Havoc in the same full-scale, life-size way as Daisy, with real models arriving on Harley Davidson motorbikes, with bangs and smoke and engines roaring, at the press launch. The only trouble was that the newspapers were dominated that morning by the terrifying Baader–Meinhof terrorist attack. The buyers were appalled. Our British manager in Hong Kong went native with a Chinese girlfriend, leaving his British wife and school-uniformed daughters in England. The seventies recession hit and buyers decided to stock one doll only: the reliable American dream, Sindy.

# Le Perchoir

MANY YEARS AGO I bought a French house that stood at the top of a village that sat on the edge of a precipice, looking down to the sea and the Var river and Nice below. The circular roads and vine terraces coil all the way down to the river. The fun is to see whether you can leap and run straight down a goat track beating a car driving down round the coiling road They practise for the Tour de France here.

The house is the highest building around and made from the pieces left over when building the church. It was originally the priest's house, so you could look straight into the campanile and make sure the bell was rung enthusiastically enough. The house had been bought by a British hero from the Fleet Air Arm of the Royal Navy after the war. He was much appreciated in the village, although one night he was so enraged by the bell ringing every half hour that he took out his pistol and shot the clock. So I bought the house without the clock.

Village life took place in the cobbled streets with boules and card tables outdoors and everyone playing a sort of whist. On the fête day in July, a vast feast was prepared and laid out for the whole village. A marquee was put up enclosing the ground floor and front door of my house as far as the village wall, with the fountain and church steps within. There was a raised platform for dancing and performing and a large jazz band. The fête went on for two days and two nights. If you went to bed the band would come into your house and play to you in bed – followed by fireworks and rockets.

The Sunday before the fête there would be a very elaborate church service. The priest would carry a cross up through the winding village to the church. Other priests and most of the children and some villagers would form a procession and follow him. Strapped to the cross would be a live rabbit. At the height of the service the rabbit's throat would be cut on the cross over the altar. No one demurred at this but they did complain that the priest always kept the rabbit to eat.

Alexander and I arrived in the village in an open-top Bentley, which was a brilliant navy blue, with nanny and baby. The village was delighted with this event – especially the car. On Sunday afternoon, after a polite request, the bonnet was opened up and most of the male population spent an hour worshipping it, with their heads in the engine and their bottoms in the air. Such is the appreciation and knowledge of motor engines in France.

Our front door was open all the time, which is not the French style, so all the children came into our house and ran about playing. They were always so polite – it was fun. On hot August evenings children are allowed up until midnight as they have a siesta in the afternoon, so ruthless games of dominos were played on our doorstep. By the time Orlando was six or seven he would sit on the steps holding court. These became regular events with rather older boys coming to play because of the ready supply of Coca Cola and Becks. They also practised their English on Orlando, reading his *Babar* and *Winnie the Pooh* books, which is not quite the way round I had hoped for.

In those days we could fly to the house for a weekend from Chelsea via Heathrow to Nice and Le Perchoir in two and a half hours, running through the airport waving our big British passports.

Josée became guardian of the house when we were not there. She owned the village shop and so dominated the village. It was said that one villager forgot to 'Madame' her and was made to walk to the bottom of the valley to buy her bread for breakfast for ever more. Josée had most things one needed, except fish, but once a week the fishmonger came in his van. This was preceded by a parade of cats through the streets stamping their feet and waving their tails. Flowerpots were not for flowers but for the local cats to take their midday siesta in.

Josée would buy you anything else you wanted when she went for the bread and newspapers in the early morning, driving her van down the mountain at Cresta Run speed. She once posted to me in England a glass jar full of black olives in olive oil, wrapped in one sheet of brown paper and a piece of string. It arrived intact.

# Sixties and Now

MEN AND WOMEN are madly fashion-conscious and aware today and very knowledgeable as a result of the web and the media. In the sixties, young people were longing for something revolutionary and new but were afraid of being sneered at or being out of step with convention – convention inevitably being the acceptable past. The easy thing was to call anything new in fashion 'vulgar'. New and vulgar are not necessarily the same thing, but it is an easy argument to make, and it caused the city gents to beat on our shop window with rolled umbrellas and complain. The newness and the subtle sexiness of our fashion made them uneasy. It was a battle. But young writers, artists, photographers, actors, architects and top models loved it, so I was not afraid of my designs being described in this way.

I see today the same frustration from young people that drove the revolution and innovations of the sixties and seventies. Today the young have consumer goods, they have food and computers and money to buy things. But young people still have no political power. They just have these pacifiers instead.

Anyone who has had children knows they only get hellish when bored, and grown-up children are the same if they are allowed to be bored and frustrated. Young men and women in their twenties and thirties are simply not listened to in today's politics.

Parliament should not be the tool of embittered middle-aged men to pad out and enrich their retirement. Young men in their twenties and thirties used to manage huge areas, larger than Surrey, in India and Africa and the colonies. They are capable of the responsibility. Young men and women should be the natural leaders in government. After all, it is the younger generation who will most suffer or enjoy the results of any political changes. Every time I switch on TV news I see international summits to be full of middle-aged men. OK, there are one or two high-profile female politicians, such as Angela Merkel or Hillary Clinton, but they are still in the vast minority. Why?

It is important, though, that power should be shared equally between both sexes. Testosterone makes men too dangerous to be allowed to run the world alone. It produces energy, drive, charisma and new ideas but it needs encouraging and directing to change focus and use its power for peace.

Men secretly love war because it proves their courage. Women hate it. Women are the great mollifiers and they provide the necessary balance. Career women have proved themselves brilliant negotiators and asset managers in the City. We need young women more than ever before to change the focus in politics, as they have done in business.

# Children

I THINK WE should teach children almost everything much, much earlier. American youth learn to drive earlier than British ones, partly because there is more space on the roads, yes, but the principle behind it is right. We need to learn languages much earlier too so that self-consciousness about accent and fluency never slows us down. We now know that people learn languages much faster as children than they do as adults.

Children are given endless computers and games but they need to be given the tools to be more creative. This might simply be a pack of good-quality colouring pencils or it might be the super new Apple machine that Hockney uses to send paintings and drawings to friends every day. This would be much more constructive and satisfying than kids sending spiteful text messages to each other on Facebook or playing computer games devised by adults, featuring stabbing and shootings.

Children should not be worn like trophies round the neck of a parent while his or her career is held back. We need skilled childcare provided by professionals, who are valued as much as professionals working in any other field.

Since women now have such a taste for independence and having their own careers as well as having children, we must be allowed to put childcare against tax. I always felt it was foolish that I could tax-deduct as many assistants for work as I thought I needed but I could not tax-deduct the most important assistant of all, our nanny. The one person you cannot do without or children go wild.

# Designers I Admire Especially

CHANEL CREATED MODERN dresses for women and made them chic – no man could do that. You had to know how a dress felt and sat and played. Jean Muir was on the right lines with her perfect black or navy dresses cut to fall between the legs, revealing a new sort of sexiness while appearing almost priest-like and elegant.

Chanel became grumpy in old age, but who can blame her: old age aches. Perfume manufacturers bullied her while the press complained she only had one idea – the Chanel cardigan jacket. But what an idea – it is forever. She had also put herself out of the game by saying short skirts were ugly because women had such ugly knees. Where was she looking? Did *she* have ugly knees? Anyway she could not and would not go back on that. But the Kaiser Karl Lagerfeld could and did. Chanel, after her death, was blessed with the greatest disciple ever, Lagerfield, who saw exactly how to do the most difficult thing: the same but different and younger.

Yves Saint Laurent's masterstroke was to reinterpret the smoking jacket for women – a permanent problem solver, with small updates to follow. We are so grateful for this and his variations on the bush jacket for urban jungle warfare.

# Birthday Treat

SO IT WAS Orlando's birthday treat. We would take all his friends from school to the theatre to see the first night of *Annie* in London. Fourteen prep-school boys, in a bus, with a driver and bus conductress. APG drew a wonderful invitation card with boys, balloons and a map for the parents to find the house. The bus had sweets and goodies on board. Mrs Nursey, aged eighty-five, was deployed to stay at South Down to welcome parents with drinks, on arrival, for the pick-up after the theatre. The buzz in the theatre, before curtains up, for a child's favoured play must be seen to be believed. No wonder actors will kill to play Captain Cook. *Annie* had the wonderful Sheila Hancock.

My anxiety was how to amuse the boys on the way back when, no doubt over-excited, they might become rowdy. Then I had a brainwave. I would take loads of bandages and plaster casts and bottles of blood. Mega success. The journey back flew by, with the boys bandaging and plastering and blooding each other.

We turned into the drive late – very late. Out of the bus stumbled limping, groaning and howling boys, hamming it up, staggering towards the front door. Inside the house: aghast parents, and Mrs Nursey blind drunk.

Me, hiding in the bus in total disgrace.

# Carpet Design

THE SUCCESS OF the furnishing fabrics for ICI led to a request for carpet design for Templeton's in the late seventies – a tempting idea. Templeton's was a very good traditional Scots company that made beautiful wool carpets. They had a huge museum studio that held the archive of their own designs, mostly William Morris-style, in complex, multi-coloured patterns – beautiful, sumptuous and, like the gardens of Versailles, only suitable to work on a massive scale and viewed from one vantage point. Delicious as the designs and carpets were, they did look out of place when accompanying ordinary, everyday life in Manchester or Bristol. The scale and overwhelming colour complexity swamped modern, fresh, Conran-designed furniture or ordinary office equipment, and didn't fit easily in a suburban house or a country cottage. It was obvious to me that carpet design, if it was to survive against the growing use of wood flooring and rush matting, must change.

So, I resisted the temptation to wallow in the wonderful Art Nouveau designs carefully kept in Templeton's archives. I saw my job as producing textured designs that would relate to modern rubber flooring or wood flooring, but with a softness of form and sympathetic colours that would work with modern furniture and the traditional mix of wood, metal or basket work. By this time I had with me, in my garage studio, three fabric students whom I had helped choose at soft furnishing company Dorma's Bursary Award.

I knew from the beginning I wanted to make a 'tweed blanket' design as the showpiece. The tweed blanket is the sampler that a tweed manufacturer produces to show all the colourways possible in a tweed pattern for the design of tweed being made. It's irresistible. One's immediate reaction is, yes, I want it all, just like that. It is like liquorice allsorts – if you fall for them, you can't think of anything else, but must have the lot. I could imagine both the colourful version of this and equally a Berber version in brown, cream, beige and stone, which could be a winner.

In our studio we set about developing these ideas on squared paper and it all went well, with ease and simplicity, which usually signals success for a project. Templeton's were enormously skilled and developed the patterns from our artwork in *pure wool*, which took the colours beautifully. The other designs were scaled versions of sympathetic textured designs that worked beautifully in classic Berber tweed colours and variations.

The collection was an immediate success. It was shown in Frankfurt, winning design awards and praise from Germany and from *Elle* in France. Magazines in Germany and France ordered enough samples to cover rooms and apartments for their photo-shoots. *Marie Claire* went mad with delight and wanted enough carpet to cover a large room to furnish and photograph in the multi-coloured design. In 1982, my favourite tweed blanket design was sold to Princess Diana for the nursery in Kensington Palace in the most colourful version.

Then came the nightmare for Templeton's, the magazines and me. The carpets were good – pure wool – but too good for the new EU anti-inflammatory regulations, which specified that synthetic fibres should be added. Disaster. The more conservative Berber colourway was sold in quantity elsewhere, outside the EU. No carpet was ever burnt.

Luckily, a certain amount had already been produced and delivered in this country, where the fire-proof rules were not so stringent. So the palace and the young princes had their beautiful woollen nursery carpet.

And though the design awards and export orders evaporated, the idea that a fashion designer could design house fabrics and textures took root.

# The Food in Nice

I AM VERY greedy, and my favourite restaurant is tucked away in Nice, in the flower and fish market. There is one restaurant that is a favourite of the market workers and the queue outside every day runs out and round the block. It is narrow and holds only about twenty tables, covered in red gingham cloth. The starter is a proper basinful of the local hand-made tagliatelle with basil, crème fraîche and freshly grated Parmesan. That more than stabilises one. You follow this with the daube (a traditional Provençal stew) and the rest of the pasta. Finally there is the perfection of little white pots filled with the darkest pot au chocolat and a small square of black chocolate served with the espresso coffee – delicious.

As you leave you will see them preparing the daube of lamb to be cooked very slowly for tomorrow, using all the remains of the local wine on the tables, left that day. It is a circular business of speed and simplicity and perfection for the people working in the market. But look out – it shuts for the whole of August, in the usual French way.

# Ferdinand

DOGS ARE A great mistake. They make a life's work out of studying how to manipulate you, and gradually take control, until they are running the roost. If you must have a dog, it is better to have two or more, so that they are kept somewhat in their place by needing to compete with each other and remember that they are dogs. Dogs quickly learn to study what you are wearing, and the time you spend on polishing and grooming yourself, in order to know how important and how long your journey is going to be that day. Their intuition is more highly tuned than ours. They learn to become your best friend and ally. In fact the uncritical loyalty is their best and most seductive trick. My favourite dog caused me the most hell.

Ferdinand was beautiful. Ferdinand was a caution. Ferdinand disrupted the countryside for miles around. Ferdinand thought his role was to serve the bitches around a ten-mile radius. Ferdinand caused the telephone wires to vibrate. He drove official dog-catchers to despair. He brought the police around and then seduced them. He brought me presents of dustbin bags from neighbours containing bank statements and credit card information, medical and dietary details – if only I had been interested. He could leap a 5'5" wall and wriggle under five-bar gates. He would not play football, only rugby, so he could grab the ball and run with it. He chased deer and sometimes won. He entered the local point-to-point horse races and disrupted everything, but again won. If I was introduced to locals they said, 'Oh – you are Ferdinand's!'

Ferdinand had a passion for teddy bears and always carried one about, which he would present to favoured visitors and policemen. He loved smoked salmon and shrimps, whiskers and all, and was rather partial to corned beef. Ferdinand ate mushrooms, not any old ones, but just the most perfect fresh mushrooms, which he sniffed out in the fields, rejecting the lesser yellow fungi and devouring only the best. He was a French black Briard and a truffle hunter: hereditary genes at work.

Ferdinand had two kennels, a winter kennel and a summer one, and slept out, protecting everybody. He was only frightened by two things – bicycles and toads – and there are rather a lot of both around my local Surrey lanes. One evening a toad jumped into Ferdinand's kennel while he was inside. This huge dog made himself almost as small as the toad, cowering and shivering with terror, while the toad whistled at him in the entrance. Both had to be rescued and pulled out. He could not resist bare, pink thighs under black cycle shorts and would give them a smart nip – not much appreciated by the cycle squadrons who raced the Surrey hills.

The British and the Germans put their trade fairs in the most unattractive places, Frankfurt and Birmingham, and then wonder why fashion people only send their assistants who only started last

Friday. The French and Italians on the other hand put their trade fairs in the most wonderful places, like Paris, Nice, Milan and Como. Needless to say I loved going to them. And needless to say Ferdinand hated it.

So, I have to leave at 5.30 a.m. for a flight to Milan for Como, the fabric fair. Rushing to grab my suitcase and my hand luggage, I find that Ferdinand is sprawled possessively on my Japanese travel bag. The bag is vital for trade fairs as it contains scissors, Scotch tape, a stapler, maps, tickets and mobile, everything I need to keep the trip on schedule, and he knows I cannot leave without it. After a fearsome tussle I make it to the car for Heathrow and the plane. On arrival in Milan, amongst a huge queue of people who take ages going through security, I idly watch the Alsatian customs dog patiently checking the passengers. I dump my Japanese sack, knowing I have to wait for the luggage. There is no point in joisting with the computer-laden businessmen charging ahead. I am surprised to see the interest the Alsatian takes in my bag.

Finally the luggage arrives and we all barge forward. I travel so much for business and trade fairs that customs men tend to know me and wave me through even when I am stacked with boxes of samples and cosmetics. But today I am halted and they pounce on my sack, rifling through it with razor blades, opening Anadin tablets with a thoroughness I have only seen with back-packers. So I apply my *Vogue* rules – sit down, cross your legs and smile, as though you have all the time in the world. I rather pointlessly add that I am not carrying anything dodgy, but all the while I am thinking, 'Oh God, I left this sack under my seat as I went to the loo on the plane. If I have been planted, I am going to miss my car, waste the day being taken apart in Milan and never even get to Como.'

Suddenly the picture of Ferdinand lusting after my bag flashes into my mind, and I ask the tough lady they now produce to strip me: 'Is your dog a bitch and is she on heat, because my dog would not leave that bag alone this morning?' Huge surprise and charts are produced that announce that Bella is 'off-duty tomorrow'. Laughter and slaps all round. I dash out to Milan looking for my driver and friend Angelo del Strada and he's waited and waited for me, so we drive like hell to my hotel, Castello del Pomodoro, where they make us a special four o'clock lunch of tagliatelli with huge shavings of truffle.

Angelo is so pleased with the sexy Bella story that he makes me promise to visit his house on the way back so I can tell it to his daughter, the doctor, who has just qualified with honours. This proves invaluable as on a later trade fair trip, the entire fashion trade and press are trapped in an avalanche of rain. No one can raise a cab. However, I telephone Angelo del Strada who dashes out at dinnertime – in Milan! – to collect me, to the amazement of all. We are true friends. Ciao Bella.

# Retailing is an Obsession

RETAILERS AND MARKETING men and women are born not made – but practice makes them as sophisticated and manipulative as a croupier.

A fashion retailer can arrange a row of scarves – as I used to – so that the next customer is bound to pick out the scarf he has decided upon. He can display a group of dresses so that a particular one will be tried on next – he devises a compulsion. He knows when a customer is seriously looking for a whole season's wardrobe on a foreign trip, even if she has dressed over-sensibly to do it, because she is that serious. He can price a customer however old her clothes and shoes.

A good retailer will use music to induce the need to buy romantic clothes or to provoke the mood to buy confidence-building career clothes. The same goes for lighting.

A retailer can always spot another retailer and will know what he is looking at and why. When a new Seibu department store opened in Tokyo, the vast queues outside to get in were televised. Nearly all were men and top retailers. Inside, all these men were stacked, one behind the other, going up the escalator. They looked like a Magritte painting. They were all professionals – you could see by the way they studied everything – and their computer brains were running that day. None of them spoke. Total recall takes energy.

Retailers are never too tall – it gets in the way and you show up too much – but they do have wide feet.

Retailers work harder than any other profession because they love it – it's a drug. They are charming and enjoy and appreciate good food and wine. Retailers are very good at poker.

Charles Saatchi is a naturally superb retailer and so are Alan Sugar and John Coleman (the former boss of Top Shop, Dorothy Perkins, House of Fraser and all). Saatchi can turn 'the world's best airline' into 'the world's favourite airline'. He knows when a brown paper bag with a string handle is more chic than a highly coloured designer bag.

# Italy

TO WORK WITH Italian manufacturers is the greatest treat. The passion for making things beautifully, plus the appreciation of all the good things in life, are two sides of the same coin for Italians. As a British designer, I could rarely have any of my designs manufactured in Britain – not even motor cars after Leyland – so off I had to go to Italy to develop the manufacture of my sunglasses designs, Venice being the centre of glass making.

Arriving in Venice I was told that Asolo was the place to go to, about one and a half hours' drive from Venice, where the best and most modern sunglasses were made. Asolo is a place of amazing natural beauty, its architecture and fabulously designed factories only adding to the beauty of the place, and a place where almost English-style gardens – semi-wild and adorned with sculptures – sit alongside their beautiful glass factories. Only the Italians could put the two together.

Italians know better than any other nation how to enjoy work. They know better than most people how to enjoy most things but when it comes to work they are the top model to learn from, always keeping an atmosphere of excitement and discovery about work and always taking at least two hours for a good lunch. If they're in a hot place or it's a hot time of year they will think nothing of having a light kip afterwards. Sunshine is to be enjoyed, as is food, beauty, work and, most of all, gardens.

In these Italian gardens, plants do not sit in tightly constrained straight lines – instead natural planting formations occur by a combination of chance and gentle persuasion. The Italians mix trees, climbers, hedges, weeds, terracotta pots, figs, grapes and gardening carts to make a blissful whole. The gardens are a microcosm of the seasons, providing perfume and wonder. I have now learnt that this idea originated in England.

That first time I go to Asolo, negotiating drawings and shapes and comparing sample sunglasses from the past with my new drawings, the meeting goes well. At half past twelve, discussions about lunch begin. The restaurant at our hotel, the Villa Cipriani, is telephoning, asking how many of us will be coming. I nervously suggest that maybe we should stick at the designs and have a sandwich sent in – but no. We leave for a two-and-a-half-hour lunch of blissful greed and rather guiltily drive back to find all the designs we discussed in the morning have already been sampled into sunglasses, in the colours and plastics and metals specified. I am amazed and thrilled. We push on with the rest of the collection until 8.30 p.m., when urgent messages start coming again from Cipriani. The porcinis have arrived, the best ever. How many do they keep back for us? The chef is passionate about these porcinis today – they are enormous. We leave for a divine dinner.

The next morning, at half past eight, many more samples have been developed ready for inspection and minute details are changed and improved for the first set. The skill and the craftsmanship are stunning. I learn that the British have long had a penchant for Asolo and have made several English-Italian gardens there. Asolo is a place where the Italian architecture, the landscape, the gardeners, the manufacturers and God are all in total design agreement.

That year we stayed in Milan in the new hotel there and discovered the Italians have not lost the ability to design and make hotels that truly work. They had realised the most important thing in any hotel is the bathroom. The bathroom was even bigger than the large bedroom and had a WC and a shower room leading off it. The bath was vast and sunken with a low seat of limestone around the edge – to receive visitors. There were teabags of delicate herbal delights to dangle in the bathtub, flattering dimmer ceiling lights and mirrors and bells for room service. Everything was absolutely right.

I remember with horror what it was to travel for work as a lone woman in the sixties, seventies and eighties. Exhausted at night after work you would eat something from room service and drink a toy-sized bottle of wine from the mini bar. Then, feeling much stronger, you would go downstairs to the hotel bar with a book to read, where you were immediately viewed as a problem. You would retreat again to your room having negotiated the loan of a hairdryer from reception, only to find it had fused.

Next evening, plucking up the courage, you would broach the dining room. A woman dining alone caused interest in most of the other guests. So I devised a game. How long would it take and which man from which party would be sent over to ask, 'Why are you dining alone?' This game demands that you order at least three

courses and the very best wine, as well as reading a book, in order
to play it correctly.

There is a hotel I like to stay at on the way to Como fabric fair.
It has the delicious name of Castello del Pomodoro. In spring you
might find a terracotta flowerpot filled with sharp green chives
growing in your bedroom, with a couple of brown-shell, hard-
boiled eggs plonked amongst the greenery. Just in case you are
overcome with hunger in the night.

The fabric trade fair takes place in Villa d'Este, the most stunning
background for anything, let alone a trade fair, so everyone in the
fashion trade loves to go. Even the food is great, and one's hand is
always near a plate of fresh Parmesan. Most of the fabric manufacturers
and printers are based near Milan and the shoe trade also meets
together in Milan once or twice a year. Italians manage to be so
passionate about their work while producing such elegance of style.
I know they worry about being cheaply copied in China, but their
ability to originate knows no bounds.

Every autumn the Milan trip to trade fares would come round,
and inevitably a fog would disrupt the return flight home. We would
often not be able to take off from Milan and would arrive in London
at 4.30 a.m. On one journey out, a very smart businessman threw a
nervous breakdown at the luggage check-in when a computer
failure at the airport had added to the chaos. He screamed and
sobbed, saying: 'She won't believe me, she won't believe me if this
happens again!'

On one of the return journeys the fog came down again, plus an
instant workers' strike further paralysed the airport. All the regulars
knew to dash for hire cars or train tickets to Trieste. I was too slow

and traumatised, but remembering the businessman's scene, I rushed to the ticket desk and hurled myself into an Oscar-winning nervous breakdown, imitating the City gent. 'He will divorce me, he will divorce me – he said he would divorce me if this happens again!' I flung myself at the officials behind the desk. Suddenly a truck was produced and I was rushed across to the take-off bay. A small British flight was held back until I was loaded on to the aeroplane and I made it safely into London. It was the last flight out.

# Formal Dress

THE BRITISH INVENTED all the great athletic games and sports. It is perhaps the best thing we have done, as it uses up excess testosterone and gives us such pleasure. Bowler hats derived from riding helmets, and evening tails were originally for hunting. Norfolk jackets were devised for huntin', shootin' and fishin'. All the garments we designed for sport moved into everyday life and finally became formal evening dress. So the effort to eliminate the tie now is rather interesting. The tie seems to have developed from the riding stock wrapped around the neck. But the tie, as worn by politicians and public figures today, seems to be something between a comfort blanket and a public penis, which you need to make sure is straight and in place before making an entrance or starting an interview. So elimination of ties would seem rather a mistake. Maybe that is where the scarf comes in, bigger and better.

After work, men tend to loosen the collar and tie to gesture: 'Job done – time for a drink.' David Cameron went to work on a bicycle in a crash helmet and full cycling rig. Will men in the future wear skinny cycling shorts, trainer boots and sleeveless T-shirts when they are at work, with hoodies (once called anoraks) or ski jackets for warmth? Probably. Men do have beautiful shoulders, so Rafael Nadal's sleeveless top plus cropped matador pants worn as tennis trousers, or Federer's handkerchief headband, may be adapted to become a more formal outfit worn for evening dress one day. Should men shave their armpits or does that make them lose their masculinity? They answer seems to be 'no' so far. Anyway, I love the look.

As a woman and as a designer I have dealt with formal dress by disobeying the rules, but using a more glamorous fabric to compensate. One hugely successful combination I discovered was black crushed-velvet hotpants worn with a black velvet jacket, black tights and boots or high heels. Black satin shorts paired with a delicious satin smock top were also a great success, as is a masculine-style dinner jacket worn with a divine white blouse, as Saint Laurent originally created and now everyone has realised. It does a lot for women. I remember being the only woman, bar one, to dine at the Stock Exchange one night, wearing my version of this style to amuse and please, noting also the exuberant pleasure the men all took in whipping off their ties, just before leaving, to say 'formality over', as well as not to be picked up for drink-driving.

In spite of this, businessmen and footballers seem to be wearing collars, ties and smart suits in a way they were not two or three years ago. So while politicians are going one way, the City is smartening up and footballers such as Beckham and Rooney and Theo Walcott are wearing classic evening dress.

As women we have fun playing with these rules but always reserving the right to wear glamorous ball gowns of immense opulence, or jeans studded with diamonds – or even a tutu over black cycle shorts. It is only fair the men should have the same fun and this is happening in design for menswear now. Many of the most exciting student graduate collections recently showed the most original design ideas for men.

Chanel saw the charm of English country clothes, perhaps partly because of her relationship with the Duke of Westminster. She based some of her ideas on this 'style Anglaise'. I loved these English traditional country clothes and fabrics, and used lots of tweeds, corduroys, Cavalry twills and Tattersall checks in my designs, reinterpreting knickerbockers, plus-fours, Norfolk jackets and riding jackets, cloth caps and so on. But I particularly enjoyed developing the shapes in surprising fabrics. My first winning garment design that I put into the shop Bazaar, I called 'pyjamas', not knowing how else to describe them. But they were knickerbockers to just under the knee, with a short curved sleeveless tunic top, in a glazed fabric with a large coin-spot print. When an American manufacturer bought this outfit along with my whole window display, he told me he was going to mass-produce the garments for the US. I was very put out about this until I had time to think about it and realise that it was great news.

British male tailors will always make shoulders masculine and square, just as French tailors cannot resist curving and slightly sloping the shoulders and implying a waist, which even for men, I love. I spent years trying to persuade London tailors to lose the strict effect and bend it. The more superficially masculine the design, the more you need to bend it. The French always knew how to cut with a curve to the bottom on pants, but the British want to flatten. Then I had the brainwave of working with American jeans manufacturers and cutting hipster or cowboy-pants style, whatever the fabric, and adding the French bottom curve to the arse – perfect.

# Colour and Fashion

COLOUR IS SO important in fashion that some of the best brains and most respected experts come together every year to contemplate and argue about new colour trends. For fashion and fabrics, for the big textile manufacturers and trade fairs, forecasting is key. Fashion designers work a year ahead but modify, add to or change their key colours completely as collections develop.

The Première Vision trade fabric show is the most powerful influence in the world of colour, but many designers will, as I do, study the forecast colours only in order to see what the mass producers will do. Therefore one can deliberately steer away from the colour combinations that will be dominating the market, knowing there will be too much of it. Colour groups can so quickly become successful, they can suddenly become an anathema and a dead duck. Yet other years, the colours are so universally 'right' and desired by everyone that there is no point in being perverse. The delight is the ongoing appetite for new colour trends. Last year's black was so right that as I write there are more than six blacks dominating the market, including deliberately bad blacks and faded blacks. There is purple-black, brown-black, navy-black, bronze-black and grey-black, not to mention the many fluorescent and matt and pearlised textures of black on top of that. Navy is almost as fluent – there are traditional Japanese navies and British navies, without getting on to sapphires, mouldy blacks, black navies, indigos and denim navies.

I love the fun names that are used for the new colours. Indeed one's choice can be influenced by a good name, so it's worth considering a colour by its code number alone, so as not to be seduced. Texture, the fabric, the surrounding colours: all completely change the look of the colour you have selected. I have always enjoyed the effect of colour on colour, and the results that the use of different surfaces and textures bring to each other. Some colours are good on one surface or fabric and not on another – they can look harsh on one and sublime on another. Then there is light. The light in different countries changes the look of the colour, not to mention the wearer's complexion.

When I am out and about I tend to pick up and carry around in my pocket or bag things that look very attractive to me, like a chestnut conker, leaves and herbs, the odd polished brass hook, or screw and rubber stoppers, just one of each because of the effect on each other. When I visit factories, I can't resist picking up from the floor bits of knit or ribbon, particularly the mesh that is often cut and filleted between one knit garment and the next. I love zips, buttons, hooks and eyes, and safety pins. I love to think about the capability of the machines as in: 'If it can do that – what about this?' Colour, like taste and smells and music, is very exciting and fluid to me. I love to walk in and out of music, say from a quiet, drowsy garden on a summer evening into a house with music playing in it. This is why I don't like music machines that require earphones. I need to be free, floating in and out of the music as I walk and feel it surround me. Colour is the same in its fluidity, relying on texture and other colours, plus the lighting around it, to achieve different effects. So I have never understood the question, 'What is your favourite colour?'

Growing up as children in wartime, coppers – pennies – were currency. A penny would be broken down, to half-pennies and farthings. A three-penny bit was big stuff. With any one of these coins enormous decisions could be made. Would you buy the black liquorice whirl, with its exciting purple jewel in the middle, the liquorice bootlaces, the acid lemon drops with sherbet in the middle, or the gobstoppers, which did stop your gob and had to be fished out at intervals to see the colour changes? Then there were jelly babies and best of all those sherbet fountains, yellow and black cardboard containers with a black liquorice straw to alternatively chew and bite, and to suck out the sherbet that choked you on the last draw. As a child one stood for hours with one's fingers just on the edge of the sweet shop counter, almost above eye level, debating these agonising decisions, while adult sales and negotiations went on over one's head.

Liquorice allsorts were the brightest sweets and prepared one for the delights of technicolour Walt Disney cartoons. So there are huge delights in cheap colours as well as great pleasures to be found in grand, rich colours and we can enjoy both. For years after the war, everyone thought in grey. In the fifties and sixties, television and cars and seemingly everything else was black and white and grey, or the very subtle watercolours of the countryside, so the shock and delight of these bright Walt Disney gobstopper colours – chrome, yellow, liquorices, black, purple and most of all orange – was very naughty.

Then colour television arrived and we all began to think in colour. Come today's high-tech computers and printers and suddenly we are all designers, using colour fearlessly and lavishly. Partly as a result, black and white is ever more powerful – both for photography and for life. A black and white composition photographed on colour film is particularly punchy.

Colour is like food: one can't keep away from it. Changes in fashion colour combinations whet the appetite in an amazing way, like chilli and cumin or Parmesan and garlic do when cooking. I have a love-hate relationship with orange, particularly the ginger sort, and I am wobbly about lime green. Chrome yellow is outrageous, although the Japanese are a bit funny about it. Yet all these colours I used in the first Ginger Group collections, probably because they are so provocative. You can't feel bored about them and they will stabilise if you use them with black and white and putty. Add an inevitably chic pruney/grape colour or a nude pink, and you are away.

The Première Vision Spring–Summer colours are wonderful this year. I would have chosen them myself, which has never happened before. I love them. It's the only time a really appealing pale pink has appeared. There is a luminous pale watery-green aqua, and an orange that screams 'Help!' Even the names are great. There must be a new team at work.

Yet all these subtleties of colour are of little import compared to the brand itself, which can dominate everything if it is successful enough.

# Some Fashion Colours

'FASHION COLOUR' IS often another way of saying you have seen too much of that colour or that combination. I then seem to go colour blind on those shades, whereas the difficult colours or combinations I had previously loathed start to become more and more provocative and exciting, and the only thing I want to use.

There are some 'can't-miss colours' like black and white – but then which white are we talking about? As soon as everyone painted their walls white and white paint colour charts came out containing such delights as floury white, apple white, chalk white, brilliant white, nougat, white mischief – well, what fun! We are not going to be done out of it.

The French take a very firm hand to green, and use it extremely successfully as a particularly sophisticated, sexy colour for evening. In Britain we have a nervousness about bright green, preferring the muted greens and browns of classic country shades. We also like the olive greens that edge towards khaki, which are traditionally British and suit us no end. We do these superbly in the 'style Anglaise'. So our tendency towards subtle greens may be to do with the idea of them suiting classic English complexions and traditions. Whatever the reasoning, faced with a strong bright green, buyers will always say to designers, 'Green is unlucky!'

Brown used to be the colour that every smart Milanese woman leapt into whatever the weather, on the first of September. It is a colour the Japanese believed they could not wear – but can. Now we all know we can wear browns with navy blues or purple or liquorice black or whatever. We simply tune our make-up tones. That dead, dark brown has a sophistication all its own that is great with a dash of pea-green.

Putty, meaning a cream with lots of green in it, is lovely and flattering with black or navy or 'ginger' orange.

Many people hate purple, saying it reminds them of the rhododendrons at their prep schools. But that must be those Surrey schools. One of my many, many schools – we moved around endlessly during the war – was in Tunbridge Wells in Kent, and purple rhododendrons for me are forever associated with fumbles in the bushes, so purple is an electric colour for me. Later I used to lunch occasionally with a famous bishop, and we would both wear purple so as not to be out-shone by the other. Purple is the most obstreperous colour especially when put next to brown or red hair, and I love it.

Kentish oast houses and the smell of drying hops on slatted floors mixed with Cox's orange apples are very provocative to me, as is the scent of chestnuts and potatoes baking in the oast-house ashes. I love the autumn colours: purple Michaelmas daisies, orange chrysanthemums, Virginia creepers, autumn crocuses, small purple grapes and tomatoes.

Orange I always see as a call for assistance, and indeed I named my orange nail polish 'Help'. Maybe this is because of the orange lifebelts they used to give you on transatlantic flights for some reason, together with a little whistle to summon aid mid-Atlantic. But not all oranges are alike: the burnt orange of Italian frescos has a different richness and calm about it.

Vermilion or scarlet red is almost as exciting as 'help' orange. Handle with care.

Yellow is another colour the Japanese think they cannot wear, but they can if they are given a sufficiently bright mustard yellow. With the right make-up it goes wonderfully with their beautiful blue-black hair colour.

Turquoise with quite a bit of sage is exciting with orange and ginger colours.

# Styling the Mini

COMING BACK FROM Paris where I had been to the trade show Première Vision, studying and buying next season's fabric, I only just managed to make the flight. Suddenly there was a sort of alert and the flight was held back. A man pouring with sweat and anxiety was hauled on to the plane and flopped down in the seat next to me. After take off and a very tense silence, he started to talk to me in the most strangely threatening way. 'I know who you are and I know where you live . . . I know you often take your son to school in the morning and clear off to the country at weekends . . . I know your nanny . . ,' On and on he went in a horrible, sinister way, deliberately trying to frighten me.

I later discovered he worked for the security company working for a motor-car manufacturer I had been to a couple of days before. He was just frightening me for fun. I suppose he was a bit thrown by being in such an incredible sweat and wanted revenge. I hated him.

Yet I was very excited to work on the styling of the new Mini car. It meant going off very, very early in the morning to the factory.

I already knew I wanted it black and white and silver. I was shown all over the factory and the production line and the pieces that made the whole. My eye was caught by some very striking black-and-white striped fabric dropped on the floor somewhere in the factory. I asked, 'Is the deckchair stripe made here? Can you make it a bit bolder? I would love it for the seats.' Well, they did and I think it made you want to leap into the car straight away.

I ordered a car for myself and longed for it to arrive. I knew I would be able to handle it so easily and those big bucket door pockets were just right. You could keep your dry cleaning, a bottle of wine, your country boots and your smart London ones in them. Not to mention the huge blocks of paper and Copic colour pens that I loved.

Alexander, hearing of my new car, promptly rang the manufacturer and changed the order from having a manual to an automatic gear box, reckoning I was such a bad driver it would be better for me. He did not tell me and I was furious but couldn't wait for another to be made, so as a result I have been stuck with an automatic gear box ever since. Anyway, I loved it and thought of it as a sort of music machine on wheels. You could park it anywhere. And Buster, my dog, looked great in it.

# Shirley Conran

WOMEN'S LIB ROSE and fell over many years, to the accompaniment of much male amusement. Many good journalists broke their backs on it, but very little progress was made. Shirley Conran, having survived the huge success of her book, *Superwoman*, plus faced down the derision of many men about life being too short to stuff a mushroom, decided to tackle the problem head-on.

Using the money she had made by amusing us, she gave a series of delicious, informative and potent lunches in one of the best restaurants, Le Caprice, in London, inviting the most influential and powerful women she knew. There would always be just two or three very intelligent and very quiet males there, but that was it.

In this brilliantly organised and professional campaign, Shirley showed these very successful women – including myself – how we could move feminism forwards. There was, of course, still much work to be done. I remember my lawyer once saying to me: 'After job interviews, we always take on the best women as they are cheaper than the men.' This may have helped a woman to clinch the job but the rationale behind it was sobering – it was not what feminism had intended!

Shirley and I had known each other through her former husband, Terence, who was terrific friends with APG from their Bryanston days. They always brought out the worst naughtiness in each other and the best laughs. Terence is a great giggler and Alexander always got him going.

Many years ago, Shirley and I took them both back to Bryanston, hoping to get Shirley's brother into the school. Having both arrived in the flashiest sports cars, roaring up the drive with squealing brakes, they then instantly metamorphosed into hopeless schoolboys, tugging at their socks and hair, as soon as they stepped over the school's threshold. Shirley and I had to deal with the whole interview with the headmaster ourselves – amazing.

# Alexander's Illness

IN 1988 DOCTORS told me Alexander would not live longer than two more years. The shock was appalling. I would drive back from the airport after a business trip to Japan to find an ambulance in the drive and Alexander going off to hospital again, sometimes two or three times a week. He said he could not live without wine and vodka anyway. OPG was a saint and escaped from school every time things were at their worst. His intuition and instinct was so strong. We had to beg Alexander to breathe, pumping his chest and giving him oxygen, which was kept at home for him. After two years, as they forecast, he just petered out.

Greatest old friends like Lindsay Masters and Antony Rouse visited at weekends as much as ever and I brought Italian food down from La Picena as before. I can't bear to write more about Alexander's exit as I will never get over it.

# Drinks with Prime Ministers

INVITATIONS TO DRINKS with prime ministers are irresistible, unless they are from Edward Heath. After my battle to cross London to the Guildhall in the worst storm of 1971, I arrived to an hour and a half wait until Heath arrived. His arrival was foretold by a booming voice that rang down the corridors, saying: 'I don't want to talk to anyone here except the man of the church.' I should have escaped there and then as this was followed up by a rambling account of his first visit abroad as a student on a bicycle and the delicious food he had experienced. This seemed to be his advertisement for going into what was called the 'Common Market' and giving away our fishing industry.

An invitation to drinks from Harold Wilson in the mid-sixties was much more rewarding. It turned out to be drinks in his tiny office alone with Harold. To my surprise, the man was utterly charming and rather flirtatious. He and I sat on the opposite sides of his desk with our elbows on board to chat. I had a glass of white wine while he had a glass tankard of what looked like beer, which he topped up regularly from his desk with a bottle of Scotch – 'The photographers, you know.'

Months later at a reception for the Soviet statesman Alexei Kosygin at Lancaster House, Harold Wilson was taking Kosygin around the guests when he nipped over to me and grabbed me, saying: 'I want to introduce you to the Russian Head of State.' With some nervousness and with the help of brilliant interpreters we chatted a bit. From then on a flood of Russian Secret Service people came, trying to persuade Alexander and me to put on a fashion show in Moscow and Leningrad. Sadly it was much too expensive for us to be able to take all the models and our collections to Russia. But a few years later in 1973, during the miners' strike that preceded Heath's Three-Day Week, the Russian newspapers came out saying that I had designed the mini-skirt to distract attention from the strike. This received enormous publicity in London and people slapped me on the back and tried to buy me drinks in a madly enthusiastic way, which was rather embarrassing being sympathetic to the miners myself. But I wish I had gone to Russia at that time.

Drinks with Margaret Thatcher were much the best. For a start it was actually dinner. One was invited alone as Dennis was not at these functions. Terribly nervous, I arrived forty minutes too early and went to the pub in Whitehall. After ordering a glass of white wine I thought, 'Better not,' and so, even after walking slowly across to Downing Street, I was on the edge of early at Number Ten when I rang the bell. To my amazement the door was opened by Margaret Thatcher herself. 'Oh Mary!' she said. 'I am so glad you came. I thought perhaps I had forgotten to post the invitations.' And there she was, bursting with pleasure at making it to Downing Street and being the first woman prime minister ever for this country. The electric shock of energy and enthusiasm that came out of her was greater than any I had ever experienced from another human being.

Dinner was with the French prime minister Giscard d'Estaing. The Common Market was being discussed so we had the most delicious Welsh lamb and mint sauce and English rhubarb crumble. British Leyland was in turmoil and it was around the time that I was in preliminary discussions about styling the inside of the new Mini car. All involved at Leyland were there and discussions were being held, to the horror and terror of a gaggle of civil servants outside the dining room door, listening in. I sat stunned with disbelief. This is how it's all done – just like that. This is how the grown-ups do it.

A few years later a newer Mini car was planned and I was asked again to design the inside styling. For this I produced an even better concept. This time I wanted to upholster the entire inside of the Mini in denim, like jeans, with top stitching and big pockets, brass studs and brass zips and so on. Unhappily it wasn't to be. As a result of the massive strikes, British Leyland was sold, the new Mini cancelled and our motor-car industry was sold off. So my denim Mini car never came to fruition and has frustrated me ever since, so I long for someone to do it, even today. It would look great.

The next time I had private drinks with the prime minister it was with John Major. He was the most charming and witty man, so alive to other people's point of view. People may be surprised to hear this, but I promise it was so. A little cabal of four of us used to go together regularly to Downing Street, one a leading woman journalist, one a major manufacturer and one a lobbyist, and me. We each came up with our own agenda for each meeting and he would listen and discuss. I think it must get rather boring and lonely in there at Number Ten, yet the bother of going out to a restaurant with all the security arrangements to be made in advance is too tiresome. In Macmillan's time, prime ministers used to just go on the underground and out to dinner at the last moment, but that can't be done today, which makes them out of touch. I found all this very interesting and enjoyable. My pitches tended to be on the need for more sports in schools and the dearth of male teachers for children today. I saw myself as light relief in this little group of four – but actually I think this hugely important.

I never had a private drink with Tony Blair, only social gatherings, but Cherie in real life has a very attractive face, in spite of the cartoons.

# Antony Rouse

'ANTONY ROUSE IS the most beautiful man at Oxford,' said Antonia Fraser, and most people agreed. He was a great friend of Alexander's, along with Lindsay Masters. Antony particularly came back into my life after Alexander died. He suggested we had some unfinished business. We had always flirted on and off.

Antony chain-smoked Gauloises and Gitanes and punctuated his pronouncements with the ash dangling precariously on the end. He wafted along and was always in love, usually with somebody new. He used to arrive at our Draycott Avenue flat in Chelsea without warning and go straight to the bookcases, taking out something obviously pre-meditated, and would promptly sit cross-legged on the floor and read for hours.

'Hi' was all you got out of him, over his shoulder. I was usually working there on my sketches and designs for the sample workroom in Draycott Avenue or the Fulham Road studio. Other days I would arrive back from manufacturers and know that Antony was there by the damp, red-spotted handkerchiefs – mine – deposited about the stairs and entrance hall. There would be wet towels in the bathroom where he had already taken a bath. The wet handkerchiefs meant he had to go back to the army for his National Service and was desperately head over heels again with a new London lover. He was always a great weeper. He rarely referred any comment to me and refused to play chess or scrabble with any woman because he 'didn't like beating them'.

Antony had an uncle who sent him whole cases of champagne and his clothes were tailor-made for him. He also favoured Brittany caps and fishermen's sweaters with tabs on the shoulders and patches on the elbows, always in navy blue. He drove vintage cars rather distractedly and devoured books on film directors, musicals, intellectuals or Proust, the latter just in case he was missing something, he said.

He was the sort of 'vegetarian' who only likes potatoes. He also ate sole meunière and corned beef but not much else. He had the most beautiful feet ever seen on man, and could beat both teams at the same time on *University Challenge*.

Antony's family lived in India and had been in the Indian Army. His parents shipped him back and forth between India and England with a nanny for the first five years, while they discussed their long-term relationship. Later his father was killed in Burma and his mother evaporated.

Antony's father's army batman in India was obviously terribly sad for him and had a pair of beautiful sandals hand-made for him and sent over to England, which took forever due to the war going on. When they finally arrived the sandals were much too small, so the last remaining present from his father could not be worn.

Antony's grandmother had brought up so many sons herself who had died in the army that she had become a bit weary of raising yet another boy. However, when Antony was six his grandmother adopted him and, becoming bored with endlessly playing snap and cowboys and indians, she gave him two major gifts to make his childhood more palatable for herself. First she bought him a typewriter and secondly she taught him how to play bridge. This was an ideal start for army life, as she knew.

The army, in honour of his father's heroic war record in Burma, paid for Antony's education, as was the army style in those days. So he was packed off to Eton, which he adored. It was Antony's first real home. There he was nurtured by his house master and his wife, who both loved him. So this was perfect. They took him sailing around Scotland every summer and would go skiing in Switzerland from Boxing Day onwards every winter, leaving behind the wrapping paper and all the Christmas rubbish – a habit of which I wholeheartedly approve.

When I asked Antony for an old photograph to use for this book, out from a very small folder fell an Eton school photo, and I realised why I was so mad about the cricketer Stuart Broad and had written a piece for a cricket magazine drooling about him. Antony was the dead spit of him.

I have since worried that my article caused Broad to cut his hair. That curly lock disappeared shortly afterwards. Serves me right, I suppose.

After Alexander died, Antony just gradually moved in. I was so used to his being around I could only be delighted. Both he and Lindsay Masters came at weekends to keep me company and Antony just stayed.

# Darcy Bussell

DARCY BUSSELL IS a dancer I have always so admired. Her name alone demands attention. It has star quality right away, plus an androgynous dash to it. Her dancing has the same attention-demanding dash. She brought ballet into this century. She abandoned those quivering, feminine, nineteenth-century gestures, and flowed with an athletic glee that takes one's breath away.

She does for female dancers what Fred Astaire, Gene Kelly and Nureyev did for male dancers. She brought to ballet a gymnastic, hockey-stick, schoolgirl healthiness, plus the grace of a panther. I have always adored ballet, but with a tiny reservation about its affectation. It is probably the other reason I wanted to do tap dancing and not ballet as a child – as well as the clothes.

Darcy Bussell has that incredible quality that only a very few athletes have. My other passion is tennis, both playing it and watching it. One player, Roger Federer, has that same amazing ability to transmit how it feels to perform at the peak of one's physical fitness through the television to the viewer. Darcy has that too. So imagine my pleasure when she stopped me in the road one day, walking away from Jasper Conran's fashion show at the Victoria & Albert Museum, and told me her mother had worked with me as a model. It turned out she was a model I had particularly admired many years ago. I was not surprised.

I am so grateful to those rare geniuses like Federer, Bussell and Astaire, who have the ability to make you 'see how it feels' and 'feel how it sees'.

# Lavergne, South-West France

SO THERE IN the estate agents' window was this apricot-pink farmhouse with perfectly placed cedars. It was low and thin with a long pigeonnier on one side. It was surrounded by tapestry-like farmland. Even the price was feasible. There was a charming woman in town who spoke English and who had once owned it and lived there. She would show us round.

Now, there was something about the way this woman walked that said 'fashion' to me. It turned out she was indeed a model who had worked for a friend of mine called Sybil Connelly, who had held my hand as I wept with fright on the aeroplane on my way to New Orleans with a party of international fashion designers including Princess Galitzine and Laetitia Crahay to accept the Best of Europe 'Rex' award.

Maria guided us to this farmhouse where, arranged outside, under a pergola, sat Madame in the perfect sunshine, reading. Three over-excited Boxer dogs leapt through the cat-flap in the front door, to see us off. The colour of the stone, the seduction of the barns and the three arches into the largest barn made the place irresistible. A swimming pool had to go there. But no, we could not see inside.

Madame lived in the centre farmhouse, her mother lived in the pigeonnier and her brother, who didn't want to sell, lived in the major west wing. Come back another day – another year. On another day the mother would not let us inside but on another year the brother was not there. So I bought it.

Maria's ex-husband, Thurloe, an Irish painter, had spent the last thirty years working on chateaux in south-west France. He was an architect with a portfolio of plasterers, stonemasons, painters and carpenters who had worked with him. He even had an architect friend who was ex-navy and an expert on drains, called Jolie, which had to be encouraging.

The roof of the largest barn had fallen in years ago and the inside was used as cowstalls, but the walls were good and the three arches entering it were lovely, making a natural walled garden in which we put the pool in the middle. The whole base being limestone rock, diggers were brought in and the pool base cut. The walls were capped and vines and roses planted to cover them.

That year, 1993, it rained in south-west France. In February it stormed, in March it showered, in April it poured, in June it deluged and in July it was still raining. In August everyone disappears on holiday. Deep trenches had been dug for drains all round the house, which now looked like the Somme. Inside the house the floor levels of every room differed, so that you tripped up a few steps or down whenever you went from one to another. I knew that this would drive everyone mad and had determined that all the floors be levelled off. Thurloe delayed starting on this and it took me several years to realise he thought, with good reason, the house would just fall down if he did this. There are no foundations on old farmhouses.

I wanted the false ceilings taken down, visualising handsome beams underneath. Well, they were there all right but they were broken and fallen down, with just stubs and holes remaining. However, the swimming pool was lovely and we stayed nearby in town, visiting Lavergne wearing farmer's store gumboots and swimming in the rain.

Four years later new beams were cut using the old boat-building technique and work started on the floor. The house didn't fall down. Vintage terracotta tiles were found and pieces of wood were inlaid between them to create a patchwork quilt effect. I had become enchanted by the Japanese pleasure in floors and the French pleasure in ceilings. The walls and ceilings were replaced and coloured and the beams were chalked. We appropriated an eye-make-up technique of using white highlighting round the tall windows. The wooden frames I wanted to be the exact shade of linen shirts when they have been scrubbed and scrubbed to reveal the colour of the natural linen yarn; the beams, the colour of the local white clay; and the ceilings milky blue. The plastered walls were to be rubbed with a pale herb green. The ceilings were very high and the beams incredibly bald so the combination of tough farm architecture in delicate wild-flower colours such as chicory blue gave the look I wanted. All the window frames, doors and shutters were made the old way by the local craftsmen. The doors were widened and lined up to give a vista through the house out to an apricot tree and pots of lavender. The kitchen was made from three rooms to form a square shape and a table was built to repeat the square in smaller dimensions, and made of local cherry. It has the local-style long drawer where bread was kept but it was all newly built by skilled local joiners and carpenters. Some of the craftsmen were old but many were teenagers, so the skills are handed down in France.

I was rather shy of rebuilding the farmhouse to this extent until I heard Terence Conran say, when asked how he had found the perfect Provençal house: 'I built it.' This is the way to get the house you want, given an architect with the know-how of Thurloe and craftsmen of such skill. Building a new house from scratch is often too demanding to visualise successfully and many an architect who builds for himself will eventually sell up and retreat to a restored Georgian classic. Total freedom is too much for most people to manage, whereas finding ways round existing faults in an old house often produces the best solutions. Use a house before you manipulate it and live in a garden before you touch it, is the best bet.

Incidentally, unlike in Britain, property is respected in France. When I was heard grumbling one day about hikers crocodiling and cycling through my land along an old, now disused, road to my pool and house, a French woman told me to put a chain and padlock on the gate of the field. When I pointed out that there was no hedge or fence on either side of the gate, she said, 'Yes, but people will know then that it is private.' So I did, and I never had anyone walk through again.

# Bathing Suits

THE TRADE FAIR for swimwear fabrics comes just after New Year, and takes place in Monte Carlo. It's lovely – you can shake off Christmas unless the fog comes down, which can happen even there. The most fun bit is that you can go by helicopter from Nice to Monte Carlo, so one year I did this and arrived slightly earlier in the evening than I expected. It seemed a good idea to have a glass of wine in the garden at the hotel at sunset.

The birds sang prodigiously and, while I was enjoying this as the evening faded to blackness, I wondered why the birdsong sounded better there than anywhere else. I then noticed there was no bird shit on the park benches – and I realised I was listening to a recording. I remembered that the Germans make recordings of the best bird songsters and play them to the lazy to bring them on a bit, and they had obviously adopted this idea here.

I thought of the nightingale that sang his heart out to us at Lavergne, my French house, through the most enjoyable dinner party one evening. I sat with a group of friends entranced until midnight, listening – all of us, just listening. It was only the next morning that, thinking about it, I realised the poor bastard was presumably reserving the right to his patch outside my dining room and kitchen, and telling us to go to bed for God's sake.

Anyway swimwear is lovely to design because the prudish bathing suit can be made even more erotic than the most ingenious midget bikini. In fact it's easier – there's more scope. The young French girl was right.

# House of Fraser

I WAS SURPRISED and delighted to be headhunted as a possible non-executive director for the House of Fraser in 1997. This was a very new experience for me. At an interview with John Coleman, the managing director, I realised he fitted the description I had written for *Women's Wear Daily* in America, which laid out my vision of what a truly brilliant MD in retail has to be and how there are never more than two or three such men at any one time. He epitomised everything I had written.

Although I had attended some fairly large board meetings before, I was pretty nervous at my first House of Fraser one. I also knew that I had to leave for a lunch appointment and not stay for the business lunch, which obviously would be an important part of my meeting the other directors. So with trepidation I apologised and explained I had to leave early, as I was lunching with Princess Diana and others, which I could not refuse. But this obviously clinched my position: 'Oh great, we'd better bring her to House of Fraser!'

The lunch was an amazing idea, which only Shirley Conran

could conceive. The meeting was to bring together six wise women: Antonia Fraser, Lynda La Plante, Siân Phillips, Shirley Conran, Princess Diana and me, to discuss with Diana what she could or should do. Shirley filled us in on the brief and we waited outside Le Caprice in the West End for Diana to arrive. The restaurant was electrified when she arrived, but being in Britain, determined not to show it. Shirley did a magnificently correct curtsey to the floor at Diana's entrance. This was after Princess Diana's divorce and although we all realised what an impossible position she was in by then, it was only when questioning and listening to her, that we discovered it was so disastrous. She was trapped. She could never take another husband or she would lose her children. Any man in the world would have lunch with her, but a full public affair, no man would dare pursue. It would be treason. Furthermore, the state would only ensure the safety of her children at the accepted royal palaces, and would not allow them to live anywhere else. So if she left the country, she would also lose her children.

Six wise women went home wiser, and so ended my first day at House of Fraser. Diana died four months later.

# Women in Fashion

WOMEN IN BRITAIN today want children as well as a career, which is difficult in fashion. The favoured career direction for women now after the first wave of emancipation is to work in medicine and the law, followed by publishing and television, which are also seen as easier careers to duck in and out of when having or raising children. Fashion is a tricky career choice for women. The ongoing obsession and intuition needed to succeed in fashion is more difficult to maintain through pregnancy and raising children. The design impact of collections tends to go off the boil during the childbearing years and business associates know this.

Being female was a great advantage for me because the twenty-year fashion period after the war was dominated by male couturiers in Paris. My success was based on designing directly for mass production, for the customer who was like me and my other art-student friends. We were the prototype for post-Pill career women to come. Couture eventually learnt from this to design for mass-market manufacturers and to design for a different, younger way of life. By the sixties young people spent most of their money on clothes.

For a woman designer, PR and promotion is more difficult to achieve when pregnant. A woman fashion designer has to be representative of her look and designs. Men can be much smaller, fatter and older than their customers or even plain odd, as they do not need to wear the model samples or look like the brand.

Manufacturers and businessmen are not usually the most forward-thinking and respectful when it comes to women's equal rights either – so it is not always a good idea for a woman designer to bounce up and make the tea or try on the samples at tough business meetings. So I think the odds are rather against new British and European female fashion designers right now. Things will change again when the many Chinese students studying at fashion schools in this country start businesses. Chinese students are instinctively good at business and in love with fashion.

China has had enormous production experience in fashion manufacturing, trained by us European and American fashion buyers, stylists and marketing experts over the last twenty years. They have tremendous experience of international sizing, taste and textiles, and international trading networks based in Hong Kong and the New Territories.

In China, manufacturers have workers sleeping on mats under their machines, working to achieve prices for European and American supermarkets – not to mention children. It is hard for other countries to compete with this single-minded determination to be the leading fashion manufacturing nation in the world.

# The Price of Fame

IN 2003 I arrived in Paris on Eurostar. A car had been arranged to pick me up to take me to my hotel for a quick dust-down and change of clothes, then to drive me to the TV studio in time for an interview with a famous French singer who had written a song about me.

As I stepped down from the Eurostar train humping my wheelie suitcase, a huge mob of British tourists going back the other way to London saw me and recognised me, and started cooing, raving and mobbing me with demands for autographs and so on. Flattered but completely enclosed by this huge group of London Limey fans, I laughed, apologising and saying, 'Thank you, thank you, but I have to get to my car and the television studio.' No way – they were a mass and would not let me pass. By the time I forced my way through, the car collecting me had given up and gone home for dinner – we were in France, for God's sake.

Outside the station there were massive queues for taxis and no taxis to be seen, so I was late at the hotel and late for the TV studios, though I did finally make it there somehow. They were all charming about it and I was so flattered by having a song written about me that I did not mind. There were lots of models produced by the studio dressed in my clothes or imitations of my designs and everyone was lovely. The delicious singer-songwriter performed, crooning his song to me. We were both overwhelmed but smiling above a large glass of delicious French wine. All was well.

So fame has its price in terms of creating panic at times but is very hard to resist. And the songwriter gave me the recording disc and I still have it. His name is Laurent Voulzy. He is charming and so is the song. As thanks I donated one of my designs to him.

# Gardening

THE MOST IMPORTANT trick for a garden is to intrigue. You need to seduce people, most of all yourself, out into the garden. What is that behind that . . . ? This is probably why I like box hedges so much. They are rich, fat and green, and behind them all sorts of excitements can sprout. Box hedges also hide things you don't want, like the prickly legs of roses. Choisya hedges are almost as good, smell wonderful and flower.

The best garden treat happened to me by chance. On my way back from Hastings art school I saw I was near Sissinghurst. It had rained all day and very early in the evening the sun came out, low and glorious across the Kent lanes and hedges. I arrived at Sissinghurst to find I was the only visitor there and I was able to walk round this magic place alone, fantasising about living there while exploring every turn. I thought about how it must have been with the Battle of Britain heroics going on above this paradise. Even having read Vita Sackville-West and Duff Cooper's diaries, I was stunned by the originality and invention of the planting. The 'Old Madame' roses sprawling up the apples trees in the long grass; the insolence of the white flower garden and the clamour of the multi-coloured garden; the avenues of the herbs that lure you on. My visit was laced with a sense of secrecy and trespass.

The most beautiful piece of land is the bit you own. There is no doubt about that. It's the trees you know that cause anxiety for their well-being, the storms you have experienced, the sunsets, the seasons, the light. I hate to miss more than ten days of it all. And yet there was a time when I remember feeling homesick as I looked up at an enormous aeroplane flying over, longing to be on one again.

But now I love the erratic shape of the fields in this country, the lack of straight lines in the planting of trees, the beech hedges, the secret rabbit warren of lanes that covers the English countryside, the luminous noisy green-on-green of the landscape and the absurd stiles, fences, and five-barred gates smothered in brambles.

My garden in Surrey was originally planted by Flora Russell, at about the same date as Sissinghurst. It is wildly unmanicured with small secret groves and sulking seats. The garden gradually goes wild at the edges where there are fields, farms and cows. I share the garden with deer and two pheasants, one called Ludovic who has eight fat wives and advertises his wares, while the females snivel in the grass. 'Shoot me if you dare,' he crows. Well, frankly I prefer the females to eat and I might just shoot one of them, but I couldn't shoot you, Ludovic, with your idiotic courage.

Alexander and I used to give autumn and winter picnics in our garden with big trestle tables spread with orange Le Creuset pots filled with daubes, to eat with pasta, plus Parmesan cheeses, nuts and fruits. We supplied huge knitted cardigans and felt hats for everyone plus electric fires with their flexes draped out of the windows. As a small boy, Orlando and his friends would join in and play 'Bang, bang, you're dead!' They had to crawl from the garden all around and make it up on to the terrace without being seen or heard, or they were dead. Alexander would have the sharpest eye and prepare himself with real firecrackers and blanks for his shotgun, which rent the air seconds before they made it. This guaranteed a long adult lunch until all hell broke loose at the end.

I like vast swags of climbing roses, wisteria, clematis and Virginia creeper, as well as hops and vines spilling out of trees and hedges. The camellias are prodigious producers because they love the cow manure and being protected from trees above. The magnolia has outgrown itself and leans into an old apple tree. And, best of all, nasturtiums grow high up through hedges with Virginia creeper behind. Chives grow between the slabs of York stone and run back under the espaliered pear trees. All is wildly out of hand because the soil is so productive and generous; it is hard to hold back. There is a yearly surprise of peonies, tentatively showing their red tips, and one blindingly perfect white lily that lives under an old rhododendron that should go, as well as some raucous fritillary that persist, making Easter every year. There is wisteria that strangles the TV aerial and the most rampant 'Rambling Rector' rose. Long grass contrasting with short mown lawns gives shape and nostalgia. Lupins in the long grass under large trees are pretty irresistible. I love hornbeam hedges with windows cut in them, and the thick dense box hedge that surrounds a circular table, making a roundel in my garden. Proper gardeners wince – but for me it is paradise. The table is balanced on a tree trunk, brought down in the hurricane. There are stone slabs under the table to place chairs, with the box hedging making a supportive back.

I love to eat things when walking around surveying the garden, so there are wild strawberries, apples, plums, figs and blackberries in abundance. I like to take secateurs to cut the one perfect rose to put in a wine glass and admire and perhaps look up its name. Usually the old French 'Madame' will throw out the odd extra perfect rose until Christmas. I also like 'Felicia' rose for her generous tumbling and most delicious smell. Choisya is my best friend here. It grows fat and delicious, flowering three times a year and filling in any clumsy gap or the back of things that I don't like. It's probably the sandy soil that makes it so amenable in England. I love the ordered, elegant look of espaliered apples along a wall but they have to be supplied by leaky hoses to support them. A line of foxgloves in front of a hedge entrance me, or hollyhocks on guard in front of a wall.

The most reliable rose I know is 'Mme Alfred Carrière'. She keeps going and going as long as you are patient enough to deadhead. In France I have this rose growing in front of a Virginia creeper, her chalky pink flower standing out in front of the lime green or dark copper. Autumn Virginia creeper on a limestone wall with dark purple clotted grapes dripping from above is pretty well delicious. Box hedging covers the worst of Madame's legs and nasturtiums, orange and yellow, scramble out from underneath. You can always eat it as well.

The Bloomsbury lot used to picnic here and were mad about camellias, but thought they had to live in greenhouses so there were not many then. Camellias have toughened up since those days and have learned to live and thrive outdoors, so I have lots of them in the garden. A secret alleyway of camellias, ten feet tall, dominates and gives mystery to the garden. How I love them – the dark Schiaparelli-pink flashy blooms, and the white ones flecked with a brush-stroke of the palest pink. I've been told this camellia has a very rude Japanese name to remind you that they came from Japan and were tea plants. The story goes that the British asked to have the very best tea plants shipped to Britain and the Japanese sent the very best tea-plant plants – camellias.

Gardens should seem to just grow the way they are and not look over-designed. There needs to be an inevitability about it – a natural quality that surmounts the whole. Like the most valuable small vineyards in France, gardens should be based on the lay of the land, taking into account where the sun rises and sets, the soil and prevailing wind.

A garden should seduce you out into it, so that you long to see what happens round the corner and to discover if there is more beyond. The Versailles approach is the worst disaster in my opinion – it is a contrived carpet design, best seen from a window inside.

A garden needs to indulge every season with a passionate flamboyance. Red, orange, pink and purple for autumn with juicy fruit berries, rosehips, hops in swags of climbers, dripping Virginia creepers, mushrooms, Michaelmas daisies and blushing roses appearing twenty feet high on top of sturdy hedges of hornbeam and box. All should be perverse, lush and surprising.

Spring is so easy – everything seems exquisite, including the weeds. But every month should be celebrated as the Japanese understand, honouring even the fallen camellia blossoms on the ground or the first weed flowering in spring. June and July is also easy with its roses, sage and wisteria.

August is my least favourite garden month, as things can look dead or tired at that time of year. But lush, sprawling, scented stock and nicotiana and tradescantia, plus well-shaped choisya and clipped box and yew, with some spectacular agapanthus in large terracotta pots, looks wonderful.

Patches of strictly mown Wilton-carpet grass, with diagonal cross-hatching, contrasted with roughly cut grass looks wonderful. I love Virginia creeper in September dripping from rampant old rhododendrons or holly, and grapes, figs and pears everywhere to eat as you go.

Claude Monet's garden is the garden to wake one up to risk. None of that faded good taste here. The trailing nasturtium on either side of the drive to the garden door is the clincher. Never again will one feel ambivalent about orange. It's the wow, help, sock-it-to-me colour, just as it is in fashion and nail polish. It is glorious bad taste, provoked by gentle mauves and milky blues with the added punch of a bit of lime green thrown in. Monet sat at his bedroom window directing the gardener to place this blob of colour here, and that there, just as he used colour when painting.

Not for me the sterile modern Babar curves of concrete walls and seats or the pebble and dried flowers of Mediterranean gardens. Give me lush, damp, green English gardens instead. So let it rain.

# The Mini-Skirt

WHAT DOES THE mini-skirt mean? I am always asked this and I often feel like I am in charge of some obstreperous child who ought to speak for herself. The sixties mini was the most self-indulgent, optimistic 'look at me, isn't life wonderful' fashion ever devised. It expressed the sixties, the emancipation of women, the Pill and rock'n'roll. It was young, liberated and exuberant. It was called the youth quake. It was the beginning of women's lib.

The mini 2012 says: 'Isn't it wonderful to be a woman? We are bigger, better, brighter and stronger and we love being female.' It suggests 'I am in charge'. It looks like 'job done' for women's lib. And the heyday for big girls — the grown-ups.

The fashion for nudity and mini-skirts seems to coincide with times of huge energy renewal and financial success. But fashion anticipates social change as much as economic change. The mini 2012 suggests the complicated nature of a woman's life today. The ruffle-frilled mini-skirt is worn with a short, sharp snakeskin jacket and a schoolmarm blouse with a fat bow at the neck that means business. Miles of perfect leg are thrust into strappy chrome mules on four-inch heels. And no doubt tiny, girly, red gingham knickers to match her red lipstick. It is perverse and schizophrenic but it is a totally accurate reflection of a woman's life today.

Thanks to the fashion revolution in the sixties and the evolution of fashion and make-up since, we now have fashion freedom. We have been taught by the fashion magazines and newspapers how to take it or leave it alone. There are so many looks and hemlines to flatter and disguise. There is no in or out of fashion – fashion is ongoing. But always just ahead of the game, desirable if you can reach it, but there for everyone to use or abuse. Fashion projects the role you want to play.

London is at the heart of this movement. Paris now appears beautiful, nostalgic and rather broke. Tokyo looks disappointed. New York thrives and London is the place that everyone wants to be.

In the sixties London was crusading on its own, but now it has become the bridge or link between Europe, America and Asia. We are the multi-cultural, multi-racial, high-tech melting pot of design, ideas and originality. We have the best fashion and design schools. London is now a world design centre. Everyone wants to work from London.

Designer fashion photographed for advertising and the net is now extraordinarily potent in influencing what we wear and how we live. Designer clothes and make-up are photographed by Bailey and Testino and digested by computers using collage and colour artifice to produce sensational effects for advertising. The result is that we want colour design editing in all aspects of our lives.

We accessorise our lives. We want aluminium chrome nails and chrome mauve lips to match the car we bought because we saw a photograph of a girl in a micro-mini in chrome mules with sky-high wedges and a mauve anklet putting her polished toes down hard on the accelerator. Virtual reality is where we live. I love it.

Women are now hairless nymphets except for the hair on their heads, which is lushly conditioned and spiked and rumpled as though straight from bed. The flesh is polished stone, the muscles trained to athletic fitness. Make-up feeds and glosses the skin while it flatters or plays surreal colour games with the face.

Women have never looked so terrific. They are six feet tall with muscular shoulders, fake buff-coloured skin and commando training. Women direct the office, organise the mortgage, plan their own pregnancy and show off the bulge. Women shop on the web and cook in the microwave. These women rule the roost. To watch Petra Kvitová or Maria Sharapova is to see that women will soon beat men at tennis.

Superwomen are the new breed. They move like athletes and sit like men with their knees well apart. Their children take their mother's surname. These awesome, gorgeous Amazons can sell their eggs and buy their sperm when needed. They are in control. Marriage is a romantic extra.

For generations the natural role for women was to be in a permanent state of pregnancy and childbirth once they were married. Countrywomen rode hard to hounds when pregnant to see if that one was a stayer. Without the strain of permanent pregnancy, women will probably become larger than men.

Now designers can work from anywhere and anytime – even amongst the mud, cows, grass and gumboots of watercolour-tinted

Surrey. However, it's the provocative chemical colours of virtual reality that dominate fashion because that's what our Apple Macs like and that decides the colours we like.

The speed of change is now from a.m. to p.m. Mobile telephones, tweeting and Facebook have cured us of any shyness. Everyone speaks on the hoof, as Americans have always been able to do. Soon it will be easy to make a slim, edited version of yourself on the computer screen wearing the fashion and make-up you like and send that to the virtual reality board meeting with virtual speech in a virtual environment. Perfect legs, perfect fashion, perfect you in a mini 2012.

# Fashion Design Today

FASHION DESIGN DOES seem the one thing we are still really good at in this country, with sexy high spirits and good nature about it. Let's support our design schools without legislation getting in the way.

# Picture Credits

*Picture Acknowledgements*

All photographs courtesy of the author with the exception of the following:

Plate section 1
By kind permission of the Mary Quant group of companies: 3 centre, 4 above; Mirrorpix: 1 below, V & A Images/© John French: 4 below.

Plate section 2
© John Adriaan 6 below right: Corbis: 3 below left (@ Hulton-Deutsch Collection); © Terence Donovan Archive: 7; Getty Images: 3 above left (Hulton Archive) 3 above right (Rolls Press/Popperfoto), 4–5 (Gamma-Keystone), 6 above left; Kensington Library: 2; by kind permission of the Mary Quant group of companies: 4–5 inset; V & A Images/© John French: 3 below right.

Plate section 3

Antony Boase: 2 above; Camera Press/Jean Pierre Masclet: 4; Corbis: 1 (@ Bettmann); Heritage Motor Centre: 3 above; by kind permission of the Mary Quant group of companies: 2 below.

The daisy device is a registered trade mark of the Mary Quant group of companies throughout the world and is used with the kind permission of those companies.

Every effort has been made to contact all copyright holders of material reproduced in this book. If any have been inadvertently overlooked, the publishers will be pleased to insert the appropriate acknowledgement in any subsequent printing of this publication.

# Index

Note: 'MQ' stands for Mary Quant, 'APG' for Alexander Plunket Greene. Entry subheadings for people are in chronological order.

modern women 192–4, 208–9,
  276–8
Monet, Claude 274
Montand, Yves 135
Moore, Dudley 54
Moss, Kate 95
Moss, Sandie 92
Muir, Jean 212

Nadal, Rafael 232
Nakayama, Juichi 176, 189, 190
Nice 219
Niven, David 135
Norman, Torquil 132, 201–2,
  203
Nureyev, Rudolf 123–4
Nursey, Mrs (South Down
  welcoming party) 214–15

Obama, Michelle 192
Okura Hotel 180–81
Oldham, Andrew Loog 57
Ono, Yoko 62
Ormsby-Gore, David 69
Osborne, John 29, 35, 58

Paris 2
Parkinson, Norman 127

Parry, Hubert 21
Penney, James Cash 67, 69
Penney (JC) 67–76
Perchoir, Le 205–7
Perelman, Ronald 115
perfume 130–33, 137
Petit, Roland 35
Phillips, Siân 264
photographers 127–9
Picasso, Pablo 135
Picker, Stanley 109–110, 115,
  137
Pill, the (contraceptive) 77
Pinter, Harold 101
Plunket Greene, Alexander
  169–70, 246; meets MQ
  1–2; jazz playing 1–2, South
  of France holidays with MQ
  16–17, 45–6; gambling 17,
  50–52; Selfridges 19–20; sells
  uncle's jewellery 20, family
  history 21–3; opens first
  Bazaar shop with MQ
  25–30; Alexander's
  restaurant 25, 34–6; marries
  MQ 37; first flat with MQ
  37–8; Knightsbridge shop
  42–4; motoring adventures